CISCO ROUTERS
FOR THE DESPERATE™

CISCO ROUTERS FOR THE DESPERATE™

Router Management, The Easy Way

by Michael W. Lucas

NO STARCH PRESS

San Francisco

Publisher: William Pollock
Managing Editor: Karol Jurado
Production Manager: Susan Berge
Developmental Editor: William Pollock
Technical Reviewers: Gordon Chan, Don Dicicco, Chris Strzelczyk, and John Mark Walker
Copyeditor: Bonnie Granat
Cover and Interior Design: Octopod Studios
Compositor: Riley Hoffman
Proofreader: Stephanie Provines
Indexer: Ted Laux

For information on book distributors or translations, please contact No Starch Press, Inc. directly:

No Starch Press, Inc.
555 De Haro Street, Suite 250, San Francisco, CA 94107
phone: 415.863.9900; fax: 415.863.9950; info@nostarch.com; http://www.nostarch.com

Library of Congress Cataloging-in-Publication Data

Lucas, Michael, 1967-
  Cisco routers for the desperate : router management, the easy way /
Michael W. Lucas.
       p. cm.
  Includes index.
  ISBN 1-59327-049-6
  1. Routers (Computer networks) 2. Cisco IOS. I. Title.
   TK5105.543.L83 2004
   004.6'2--dc22
                                            2004013809

DEDICATION

To all those poor bastards who are awake at oh-dark-thirty trying to get their router working.

ACKNOWLEDGMENTS

Special thanks go to Chris Strzelczyk, Gordon Chan, and Don Dicicco. Also, as always, to Elizabeth Lucas, for not smothering me in my sleep as I was working on this book.

BRIEF CONTENTS

CONTENTS IN DETAIL

CHAPTER 4
WIDE AREA NETWORK CONNECTIONS 33

CHAPTER 5
TROUBLESHOOTING ROUTERS 49

CHAPTER 6
IOS CHANGES 67

CHAPTER 7
REDUNDANCY WITH BGP AND HSRP

CHAPTER 8
LOGINS, AUTHENTICATION,
AND REMOTE ACCESS

CHAPTER 9
CISCO NETWORK SERVICES

INTRODUCTION

Welcome to *Cisco Routers for the Desperate!* While network administrators know that they should intimately understand every piece of equipment on their networks, in the real world we all become most familiar with the things that require the most care and feeding. We all spend more time than we'd like arguing with buggy operating systems and applications, and as a result are very familiar with them. Cisco routers "just work" almost all the time, so we don't get much chance to become familiar with them. This gives the router a certain air of the "mysterious black box."

When the router actually breaks, the mysterious black box immediately becomes an object of fear and dread. The fight-or-flight instinct kicks in, people panic, and pretty soon everyone's running around as if they have a drunken badger loose in their undies. Perhaps you call your Internet service provider and beg for help—always a legitimate tactic, but perhaps not the quickest and certainly not the best for your self-respect. You could go buy a book on Cisco routers, but most of those that actually contain useful information weigh roughly the same as an automobile transmission and are almost as digestible. And we all know you won't have time to get through it during an actual emergency, will you?

This book is aimed at the administrator of a small network who is responsible for anywhere from one to three Cisco routers. Our goal is to make you comfortable with the Cisco environment and provide exactly the information you need to troubleshoot and resolve the most common problems that either happen on Cisco routers or intimately involve Cisco routers. Once you have that under your belt, we go a little further and provide the basic information you need to address some of the questions that frequently arise when working with Cisco routers and network connections. This book is also short enough to actually be read.

This is the book I wish I had read before I first touched a Cisco device.

This book is not a complete tutorial on all of the things that can be done with Cisco routers. Cisco almost invented the networking business, and its equipment has been used to interconnect almost every sort of network hardware ever created. We focus squarely on TCP/IP networking in an Internet environment and do not detour into channelizing circuits, VoIP, IPX, AppleTalk, or any of the other features available in Cisco-land. Instead, you'll discover how to learn these things yourself. Once you're comfortable with Cisco routers, everything else follows.

What This Book Will Teach You

The main goal of this book is to make you comfortable with the environment and technology found inside every Cisco router. First, you have to connect to the router and log in, and we'll discuss how you can do that. You also need to examine interfaces, check the configuration, and change the system's current and startup configurations as well as run some basic troubleshooting commands.

To make the router work properly, you'll need to have a basic comprehension of the network types most commonly found on modern TCP/IP networks. We'll briefly cover

Ethernet and serial lines, and we'll give some pointers to further information. This isn't a primer on networking, but you need to understand enough theory to comprehend router error messages.

We'll then discuss the most common router usage, connecting a small network to the Internet. We'll go step-by-step over the typical configuration choices, and then learn how to preconfigure a router so that you can quickly and easily set up a connection with a minimum of fuss. This will allow you to ask your ISP for the specific information you need, rather than their telling you what you need to type. To make your Internet connection work, you'll also have to configure the router's Ethernet interface, so we'll discuss that as well.

Perhaps the second most common use of a router is to connect two offices with a private leased line. This is a step up from connecting a network to an ISP, and we'll cover how to make this happen, beginning with ordering the circuit from the telephone company. Because you'll be responsible for this circuit, we'll cover troubleshooting as well.

As good as Cisco equipment is, its products require occasional software updates to solve stability and security problems. We'll take you through doing this safely and reliably, and we'll discuss recovering from the most common problems.

Whenever the office Internet connection goes down, managers all have the same question: "What would it take to get redundancy?" We'll unveil the mysteries of BGP, the Border Gateway Protocol, and show how you, as a small network provider, can use BGP to provide some measure of network redundancy. We'll also discuss the problems associated with BGP and some workarounds that can solve those problems.

Finally, Cisco routers can take advantage of a variety of network services that you might already offer, and they offer other interfaces to more easily fit with your network. These include such basic protocols as SSH (Secure Shell), NTP (Network Time Protocol), and SNMP (Simple Network Management Protocol). We'll briefly discuss how to configure these and others.

Where You Can Learn the Rest

If you need more information, it's available elsewhere for either a small fee or at no cost.

By far, my favorite source of information on a Cisco problem is the Google search engine. Usually, a quick web search with well-chosen search terms will give an answer on the first page. The problem, of course, is finding those "well-chosen search terms." Usually, the word "Cisco" and a snippet of the technology or error message will suffice to provide an answer. Be sure to check both the "groups" and "web" search functions, because Google indexes the entire history of Usenet (including even the early days of Cisco).

If you're a Usenet (aka "Internet News") user, check the newsgroup comp.dcom.sys.cisco. While this group hasn't had a FAQ update in several years, it's still actively used and is an excellent place to get pointers to further information on almost any Cisco-related topic.

By far, the most authoritative information on your router is available on the Cisco website, http://www.cisco.com. Documentation for all router models, modules, and other hardware appears there along with tutorials for configuring features specific to each model or module.

Although all of the above-mentioned items are free, I cannot recommend a Cisco SmartNet contract strongly enough. The cost is small compared to the cost of the router, and having a contract ensures that a Cisco engineer will immediately be available to you whenever a critical problem occurs. If you have to resolve a router problem on your own, you may find yourself struggling for hours or days. But if you have a contract, your service might well be restored within minutes of a simple phone call. The cost of downtime when you're struggling with a problem on your own almost certainly far exceeds the cost of the SmartNet contract.

Additionally, Cisco tends to very quickly respond to low-priority Technical Assistance Requests that SmartNet customers can enter on its website. I've come to expect answers within an hour on even trivial questions, and have never waited more than a day. While Cisco does not guarantee this level of service, rapid response is very routine for them. You can spend far longer than that hunting for answers on the Internet.

Unpacking the Router

If you're lucky, your first introduction to Cisco routers will be a brown box arriving on your loading dock. This means that you'll learn how to configure the router by actually installing it, which is much easier than having to thoroughly understand a working setup. If you aren't this lucky, just pretend that your server room is a really *big* brown box and follow along. You may have to search the office for the where your predecessor stashed some of the router accessories, but at least you'll know what you're looking for!

While the most interesting part is probably the router itself, be sure to find the console cable and adapter as well as the manuals and CD-ROMs. In a modern Cisco router, the console cable is usually a flat blue cable with an RJ-45 connector on each end and an RJ-45–to–DB-9 adapter to let you attach to the serial port on your computer. Hang on to this cable, because you will need it later. (Because Cisco console cables tend to wander off if left unguarded, I keep a spare locked in my workshop in a fireproof safe labeled "Caution: Live Plague Virus.")

The manuals are generally available on Cisco's website if you have a SmartNet contract, but a paper copy is nicer to read while sprawled on the couch. Many modern Cisco routers are *modular*; the router chassis has several slots where cards containing connectors for different types of networks can be plugged in. Each card or component has its own manual. While we will cover basic configuration of the most common network interfaces, you should definitely check the manual for any special requirements for your modules.

Lastly, the CD-ROMs contain router software, additional documentation, and add-on tools that can help you manage your router. Keep this software, it can help greatly in disaster-recovery situations.

Break out the router chassis manual and look at the router itself. Things you should look for include the console port, the aux port, and the network interfaces. Let's start with the console port.

WARNING   *Do not power your new router on yet!*

Console Setup

Your Cisco router has a port resembling a standard Ethernet RJ-45 port, labeled "console." You received a console cable with your router; plug one end into your router and attach the serial port to a 9-pin serial port on a computer.

Now you need serial port client software on your computer. We'll assume that you're using HyperTerminal for Windows to connect to the router. HyperTerminal is available on all versions of Windows. If you're using another operating system, it must have a serial port program available. Free Unix-like operating systems usually include "tip" or "cu," and "kermit" and "minicom" are also available for many different operating systems.

I frequently use a serial cable and a VT100 terminal emulator to console into a router from my handheld. (Handheld devices are an excellent choice of console client in crowded server rooms where the narrow space between racks make managing a laptop difficult.) Specifics of configuring these programs vary, but the settings we use here will work for any of them.

In modern Windows versions, HyperTerminal may not be installed by default. If you look under Start > Programs > Accessories > Communications and don't see HyperTerminal, it's not yet installed on your system. Go to the Add/Remove Programs control panel and select "Windows Components." HyperTerminal is part of the "Communications" feature set.

Once you have your serial client software installed, set up a new connection to your serial port. Use the following settings:

9600 baud

No parity

8 data bits

1 stop bit

No flow control

Click the "connect" icon. Because your router has no power yet, you shouldn't see anything happen.

Other Router Ports

The aux port looks just like the console port, and you can even plug in your console cable and get a command line on your serial client. The router doesn't display its bootup messages on the aux port, however. For the most part, the aux port is there only in case something goes wrong. If you misconfigure your console port and find yourself locked out of the system, you can log in via the aux port and fix the router's config-uration. In the event that you really botch an upgrade, you can set your aux port to use a high-speed connection and upload a new software image to the router over it. You might connect a modem to your console port for remote work, and use the aux port for local work.

Network interfaces look different from router to router, but for the most part they have a connector appropriate to the type of network they connect to. Ethernet interfaces usually have either a standard Cat 5 or fiber connection, while T1 interfaces look like Cat 5 connectors. Larger circuits, such as DS3s and

OC3s, have coaxial connections. Look at your router and identify the type of network interfaces it supports; you'll need to know that later.

Power-On

With your serial connection in the console port, plug in the router and in a few seconds you'll see some activity.

```
System Bootstrap, Version 12.2(1r)❶ [dchih 1r], RELEASE SOFTWARE (fc1)
Copyright (c) 2001 by cisco Systems, Inc.
C7200 platform with 131072 Kbytes of main memory ❷

Self decompressing the image : ######################### ❸
...
```

You'll see a variety of facts about the equipment, such as the ❶ boot loader version and the ❷ hardware platform. The system then starts ❸ loading the operating system and heads for the main boot sequence. We'll see how to interpret most of the output it gives later in this book. Let it keep going until it wants to talk to you. If this is the first boot, it will offer to let you configure it:

```
Would you like to enter the initial configuration dialog? [yes/no]:
```

The configuration dialog is designed to get a bare minimum system up on the network, allowing you to use a configuration tool such as CiscoWorks to complete the setup. For reasons we'll discuss shortly, I encourage you to perform all the configuration at the command line instead of via one of these tools. (Once you've read this book and understand the implications of your choices, you might want to use the configuration dialog to perform basic setup.) For that reason, I recommend that you skip the configuration dialog. This will drop you to a router prompt.

```
Router>
```

Congratulations! You're now actually logged in to the router. Now, let's see what you can do with it.

1

BEFRIENDING
THE COMMAND LINE

This book focuses entirely on the command line. Why? Some Cisco routers include a web interface; others don't. Cisco sells advanced router management packages, but they require a complicated client environment that you might not have available when you really need it. You might only need to log in to the router once a year or less; what are the chances that your desktop system with all the fancy management tools has undergone some drastic surgery in the meantime, and the router tools no longer work the way you expect? Personally, I dislike trying to solve Windows problems when the router is down. The one environment available on every Cisco router is the command line.

The command line gives you absolute control over every aspect of your router's behavior. Some configuration changes can only be realistically made at the command line. If your router loses its configuration, you'll need to use the command line to restore enough of its mind that your fancy tools can talk to it. So, if you must use the command line in those desperate circumstances, it's best that you learn enough to be comfortable there.

EXEC versus Privileged EXEC Mode

By default, when you first log in to a Cisco router you are in *EXEC mode.* You can execute basic diagnostic commands and look at things, but you cannot actually change configuration settings or view sensitive information. For example, in EXEC mode, you can see if an interface is receiving errors, and you can ping across a circuit to see if it is working, but you cannot reset the interface. In EXEC mode, the command prompt ends in a "greater than" sign.

```
Router>
```

To change anything, you must be in *privileged EXEC mode,* which is a superuser or administrator security level protected by a unique password. Privileged EXEC mode is sometimes called "enable mode." In enable mode, you can configure the router in any way desired, reboot the router, or take any other action possible in the software.

To enter privileged EXEC mode, use the `enable` command. When you actually have a password set to access enable mode, the router will prompt for it when you try to enable. See the "Passwords" section in Chapter 8.

```
Router>enable
Router#
```

In enable mode, the command prompt ends in a pound sign.

The old method of Cisco access control was to give the standard EXEC password to all the technicians but restrict the enable password to the senior techs. Setting up discrete usernames is a better way to achieve a similar effect, but many older routers still only use unprivileged and enable passwords—either because they haven't been updated, or because that's all that they can support. There's nothing wrong with restricting the use of privileged mode in this way, especially in a small shop where only one or two people connect to the equipment, but if you have more people you'll probably want to set up separate usernames and allow individuals to be privileged or not. We'll see how to do this in Chapter 8.

Integrated Help

"Help" might be too strong a word, but routers give hints on commands, command syntax, and the features available in the router. Different versions of the Cisco IOS have different features, and it's not easy to identify them all. The simplest way to see what commands are available is to ask the router. Once you've logged in, enter a single question mark at the command prompt.

```
router#?
Exec commands:
  <1-99>        Session number to resume
  clear         Reset functions
  clock         Manage the system clock
...
```

My test router has four full screens of commands available from a single question mark. Many of these commands are completely irrelevant for a router that is providing basic Internet capability; such activities require only a very small subset of Cisco's features. Still, this can be a helpful reminder when you can't quite remember the name of a particular command.

You can request hints about individual commands. Many actions require one or more words to complete, and Cisco's integrated help system will provide helpful reminders about syntax or required information upon request. For example, the show command is used to view system information. If you want to know what arguments a show command can take, ask the router by entering show ?.

```
router#show ?
  access-expression   List access expression
  access-lists        List access lists
  accounting          Accounting data for active sessions
  adjacency           Adjacent nodes
...
```

On some versions of the IOS, this output can go on for screens and screens. If you know the first part of a command's name, even just the first letter, you can narrow it down by giving what you remember of the command and a question mark.

```
router#show a?
access-expression  access-lists  accounting  adjacency  aliases
alps               arp           async
router#❶show a
```

Note that on your next command-line prompt, the router automatically prints the ❶ chunk of command that you gave before the question mark. The system knows that you want to type something that begins with show a, and is trying to make it easier for you.

One thing to remember is that hints on a particular command are only available in the mode in which the command is available. For example, the commands beginning with ip, such as ip route, are only available in enable mode. Entering ip ? in standard EXEC mode will generate an "unrecognized command" error.

Command Abbreviation

One interesting feature of the Cisco IOS is that it allows the user to abbreviate command names to the shortest unique abbreviation for a word. For example, one common command we'll use again and again to view settings is show. If you ask your router for all the commands beginning with the letter s, you'll get a whole list.

```
router#s?
❶*s=show  sdlc  send        set     setup
❷show     slip  start-chat  systat
router#
```

Note that only the command ❷ show begins with the letters sh. You can use the letters sh as an abbreviation for the full word show; the router is smart enough to know that you couldn't possibly be typing any other legitimate command that begins with those letters. In this particular case, the letter s is also ❶ specially marked to indicate that it is an abbreviation for show; apparently Cisco thought that show was so commonly used that it made sense to abbreviate it further.

In this book, we will give commands in the text by their full forms. Example commands may be in abbreviated form if they are commonly used that way.

2

ROUTER CONFIGURATION

Now that you're logged in, let's set up the router. The show version command explains some basic facts about your router, such as the software version, hardware type, and supported interfaces. Because the output is quite long, I won't include it all here, but we'll look at a few important snippets.

```
router#show version
Cisco Internetwork Operating System Software
IOS (tm) ❶3600 Software (C3640-IS56I-M), ❷Version 12.0(7)XK1,
EARLY DEPLOYMENT RELEASE SOFTWARE (fc1)
...
```

The second line gives you the ❶ hardware platform this IOS is
meant for and its ❷ version number. If you have to contact
Cisco, you will need to provide the version number. Next are
details about who built this software and when, the ROM
version, and so on. While Cisco would certainly want to see all
of this information if you called for support, you can't do much
with it by yourself.

```
...
router ❶uptime is 4 weeks, 4 days, 9 hours, 53 minutes
System returned to ROM by ❷reload
System image file is ❸"flash:c3640-is56i-mz-120-7-XK1"
cisco ❹3640 (R4700) processor (revision 0x00) with 123904K/7168K
bytes of memory.
...
❺4 FastEthernet/IEEE 802.3 interface(s)
6 Serial network interface(s)
...
❻Configuration register is 0x2102
```

The ❶ uptime tells how long the router has been running
(4 weeks, 4 days, 9 hours, and 53 minutes), and the next line
explains ❷ why it last went down. (A *reload* is a software-driven
reboot, as we'll discuss in Chapter 5.) When a coworker asks,
"Are we having Internet trouble?" it's nice to be able to say that
the router has been working all along.

The ❸ system image file (in this listing, "flash:c3640-is56i-
mz-120-7-XK1") is the location and name of the file that the
router loaded as its operating system; this information will be
important when the time comes to upgrade your IOS. The ❹
model information and physical characteristics of the router
(shown below the system image file) can be important; if your
router is in a remote office, looking at this information may be
the easiest way to learn what sort of equipment it is. (It would
have been even easier for you to document the router before
sending it to the remote location, but generally it's easiest of all
to just ship it and forget it.)

After a few more lines that detail software features, we'll
see the ❺ interface types installed in this router. The router

will then list some model descriptions for components and end with the ❻ configuration register (which probably means nothing to you right now but will be important during IOS upgrades).

Running versus Startup

A router has two configurations at any given time: the *startup configuration* and the *running configuration*. The startup configuration is stored in the router's nonvolatile memory and is used to configure the router during the boot process. At that point, a copy of the startup configuration is placed into the running configuration. If you change the router's configuration during operation, you're changing the running configuration. When you save the running configuration, it overwrites the previous startup configuration and becomes the new startup configuration. If you do not save your changes before you reboot the router, the changes are lost.

NOTE *This is a long-winded way of saying: save your changes or you'll lose them at the next reboot! Changing a router configuration is no different than editing a document in a word processor; if you exit without saving, you lose your work. This can be good or bad; don't be afraid to use this to your advantage if you really screw up your router's configuration!*

Technically, you could say that the startup configuration is a configuration file; it's stored in nonvolatile RAM, just like a file on disk. Cisco experts don't generally refer to the startup configuration as a configuration file, however; it's just a "configuration." The running configuration is certainly not a file; it's a (possibly modified) copy of the startup configuration, held in memory.

Startup Configuration

To view the configuration the router will boot with, enter the show startup-config command.

```
router# show startup-config
❶Using 5620 out of 129016 bytes
!
❷version 12.0
...
```

The router reads the configuration from permanent storage and ❶ tells you how much space it takes up before displaying the ❷ configuration proper.

Running Configuration

To view the current (running) configuration, enter the show running-config command.[1]

```
router#show running-config
❶Building configuration...
❷Current configuration:
!
version 12.0
...
```

Note the first line of the output, where the router tells you that it is literally ❶ assembling the current configuration from the router's memory. It then ❷ reminds you that this is the configuration in memory at the moment, which may or may not match what is in NVRAM. It then displays the configuration one screen at a time.

Reading a Configuration

We won't dissect a single complete router configuration in this book, because a working configuration for even a small router can easily reach up to 200 lines. Here's how to read this configuration, though.

A Cisco IOS configuration consists of a series of statements. Each statement either activates or deactivates a feature for an interface, a protocol, or the router as a whole, or defines some global characteristic of the router. You'll also see exclamation points, which IOS uses to separate sections of a configuration. (If you store copies of your router configurations in a place other than on the router, you can use exclamation points to indicate comments, much as the pound sign is used by many program configuration files. This is rarely done, because the router will strip out these comments when loading the configuration.) For example, here are some snippets of a small router configuration file.

---

[1] Old Cisco farts may remember this as write terminal or wr t. There's nothing inherently evil about wr t, but it's considered obsolete.

```
...
❶service timestamps debug uptime
❷!
❸hostname router.blackhelicopters.org
...
```

This router supports the ❶ network services timestamps, debug, and uptime. (Just listing them in the configuration file is enough to enable them.)

We also have a global configuration variable, the ❸ router's hostname. If the router thinks that configuration sections are sufficiently different, it puts a ❷ blank line between them.

```
...
❶ip subnet-zero
❷ip domain-name blackhelicopters.org
❸no ip finger
...
```

This router has two settings for Internet Protocol (IP): the ❶ subnet-zero feature is enabled, and the ❷ IP domain name is set. Conversely, the "no" setting disables a particular service; in this case, the ❸ finger service is turned off.

```
...
❶interface Serial1/1
❷ description main office T1
❸ no ip redirects
...
```

Here we have a configuration for a ❶ particular router interface. Configuration information for this interface appears ❷ directly beneath it and has a single space in front of it. Note that we specifically turned off ❸ a particular IP feature here, ip redirects; we could enable this feature on the router as a whole and then disable it on an interface-by-interface basis.

```
...
❶router bgp 8292
❷ bgp dampening
...
```

Similarly, ❶ major routing protocols configured on the router each have their own section. Configuration for that protocol (dampening) appears ❷ directly beneath it, set off by a leading space.

Configuring the Router

When you're in privileged EXEC mode, you can not only issue more powerful commands but also change the router's configuration.

To change the router's configuration, you must enter *configure mode*. The most common way to configure the router is at the command line you're logged in at, also known as the *terminal*. Enter configure terminal at the privileged mode prompt.

```
router#conf t
Enter configuration commands, one per line.  End with CNTL/Z.
router❶(config)#
```

Note that the ❶ command prompt has changed from simply router to router (config); the router is making it explicit that you are configuring the system. At the configure prompt, you can enter configuration statements, one statement per line.

Configuration commands look exactly like those in the system configuration and are added directly to the router's configuration. For example, to add the line service password-encryption to your configuration, just enter it at the configure prompt.

```
router(config)#service password-encryption
```

The router will place this in an appropriate spot in the global configuration. (No, you can't put the statement in a place of your own choosing in the configuration; the router knows far better than you do where each line belongs and will blatantly ignore any attempts to reorder the configuration.) Entering a command like reload or ping at the configure prompt will only generate an error, because these are not legitimate configuration statements.

When you have completed your configuration, leave configuration mode with CTRL-Z.

```
router(config)#^Z
router#
```

The prompt changes back to simply router.

Configuring a Particular Interface

When you need to configure a particular interface, just enter the interface name at the configure prompt. The router will place any further statements under the interface configuration.

```
router(config)#int s1/0
router❶(config-if)#
```

Note that the ❶ prompt changes to `router` (`config-if`) to remind you that you're configuring an interface, not the entire router.

Why is this important? Do you remember our example configuration that had `no ip redirects` on a single interface? Presumably that router needed the feature enabled on some other interface or on a global level, and it would have been enabled that way.

Routing protocols have a similar configuration sub-prompt.

```
router(config)#router bgp 8292
router(config-route)#
```

Any further statements will appear in the `router bgp 8292` section, as shown in our example earlier.

Saving Changes

Entering all these configuration statements will alter the running configuration, but that configuration won't persist through a reboot unless you save the configuration. Use the `write` command to save your changes.

```
router#write
Building configuration...
[OK]
router#
```

Backing Up Router Configurations

There's nothing particularly special about router configurations; they're just plain text. The simplest way to back up your router's configuration is to copy the configuration statements to another system, perhaps a plain text file on a server or even to a piece of paper in a logbook. Should your router suffer a critical failure and lose its mind, you can restore service by just going into configure mode and pasting in the entire router configuration.

It is also possible to copy your router's configuration to an FTP server with the copy ftp command. The process is quite similar to the FTP process used for IOS upgrades, and it is an *excellent* precaution to take before an upgrade, so we'll discuss it in Chapter 6.

3

ROUTER INTERFACES

One of the main functions of a Cisco router is to connect different types of networks. Connecting Ethernet systems together is quite straightforward, and connecting WAN links together is just as easy, but these two very common network types simply refuse to talk to each other without an intermediary. The router allows you to treat very different physical networks as a single continuous entity.

Cisco routers support almost any type of network interface: Ethernet, serial, token ring, DS3, OC3, asynchronous modem, and so on. These interfaces might be on add-on cards that slide into a system much like those used in a laptop, or they might be integrated with the system. And when some bright scientist develops direct neural links into the human mind, Cisco will have an interface for that, too. But until then, Ethernet and serial are the most common interfaces, so we'll focus on them.

Got Interface?

Cisco devices can display information about each interface attached to the system. By looking at the system interfaces, you can see not only what sorts of interfaces the router has, but also how much traffic each interface is handling, what sort of network errors the router senses, and a whole slew of further detail about the networks the router is attached to. To see every interface on your router, enter "show interfaces" (sho int). Every interface on the router will show up with an entry starting like this.

```
router#sho int
❶FastEthernet❷1/0 is administratively down, line protocol is down
  Hardware is AmdFE, address is 0003.e35e.d191 (bia 0003.e35e.d191)
...
```

Routers list their interfaces by their internal order in the system. At times this order will be clearly labeled on the outside of the system, while at other times you might wonder where the router learned to count.

Each interface is uniquely named by a ❶ type (FastEthernet in this example) and a ❷ unique number for that type (1/0).

The first interface of any type is numbered 0. A split number like the one in this example tells us that multiple interfaces are loaded into a single add-on module. For example, the interface FastEthernet 1/0 is the first Ethernet interface on add-on card 1. If this add-on card had a serial interface as well as an Ethernet interface, you could also have Serial 1/0 show up. Numbering all depends on how the router thinks the interfaces are attached.

On a router with many interfaces, you might only want to see a particular interface. For example, if you want to see if your Internet circuit is working, you only need to look at the interface that's connected to that circuit, not every interface on the router. To display a particular interface, add its name to the sho int command. For example, to see only the interface serial 0, enter sho int serial0.

As with commands, you can abbreviate interface names to the shortest unique identifier: these abbreviations usually contain just enough letters to uniquely identify the interface type and number. For example, serial 1 can be s1, ethernet 0 can be e0, and fast ethernet 2/1 can be faste2/1. Have a look at your router's interface names to see how they can be abbreviated.

Common Interface Characteristics

When you run sho int on most types of interfaces, including serial and Ethernet, you will see a great deal of similar information in the resulting output for each. The example below shows the first part of sho int output for an Ethernet interface, but everything we'll discuss relates to serial interfaces as well.

```
router#sho int fastethernet2/0
FastEthernet2/0 is up❶, line protocol is up❷
  ❸Hardware is AmdFE, address is 0003.e35e.d1a1 (bia 0003.e35e.d1a1)
  ❹Description: Main office Ethernet hub
  ❺Internet address is 198.88.118.129/25
  ❻MTU 1500 bytes, ❼BW 10000 Kbit, DLY 1000 usec,
     reliability 255/255, txload 1/255, rxload 13/255
  ❽Encapsulation ARPA, loopback not set
  ...
```

The output for each interface continues, but it's mostly debugging information and not useful at the moment. We'll look at that additional output in Chapter 5.

Looking at the output above, we first see that this interface is ❶ up. This means that a physical cable is plugged into the interface and that the router sees a signal being sent over it that it can understand. If the interface is unused or empty, or if there is some physical problem with the circuit, the status would be down. If your interface is up, chances are good that there is no physical problem with this network; if it is down, the problem can quite possibly be identified by walking along the wire looking for problems.

Next is the ❷ line protocol status. The line protocol tells us the encoding used by the signal coming over the line. Every network type uses some sort of physical protocol that encodes the actual data into a string of ones and zeros. As long as the devices on the other end of the wire use the same protocols as the router interface, this line should read up. However, even if you have a working circuit plugged into your router interface, if the routers on either end are using different line protocols, the status here would read down. You must have both an "up" circuit and protocol agreement to actually use the circuit. If your circuit is up, but your protocol is down, your configuration is probably wrong at one end or the other. The line protocol is set in the "encapsulation" section (described in point ❽ below).

The interface reports the sort of ❸ hardware this router is using for this connection. This name is frequently some obscure Cisco internal part number or name, but it might include a description of the part. Unfortunately, there is no publicly accessible master list of these parts, but if you are familiar with the technology, you might be able to glean some useful information from the hardware description. In this example, we have the Fast Ethernet port's MAC address.

You can enter whatever you like in the ❹ Description field. While this might seem pointless for a usual SOHO network with just one interface, it can be very helpful to enter a plain English descriptive name here when your router has multiple interfaces of each type. On serial circuits such as T1s or DS3s, I recommend putting the telco circuit ID in this field. (We'll discuss circuit IDs in Chapter 4.)

Every configured interface has some basic ❺ TCP/IP configuration information, such as an IP address and netmask. (We'll see how to configure this later this chapter.)

Next, we have some basic information about the ❻ physical protocol spoken on this interface. The standard MTU (Maximum Transmission Unit) for most devices on the Internet is 1500 bytes, as shown here; if yours is different, someone set it that way for some particular reason. Changing this value will probably increase the fragmentation of packets that pass through your network and is generally inadvisable. (If your MTU isn't 1500 bytes on an Ethernet or T1 circuit, that's almost certainly your problem.) Big circuits such as DS3s and OC178s have their own proper MTU values, and mucking with them will cause all manner of difficulties.

The ❼ BW value is the total bandwidth of this interface. This can be vital information if you're trying to determine why your router seems to be slow. If your router can handle 10,000 kilobits per seconds (like this interface), and you want to cram twice that amount through your network, you're going to have serious problems.

Finally, the ❽ encapsulation is the logical protocol used for this interface. In the most basic sense, this tells the router what sort of network you're attached to. In this example, we're using ARPA encapsulation, which is used for all Ethernet interfaces. (Serial links have more options, as we'll discuss in Chapter 4.) This is where the "line protocol" discussed earlier is set. If your line is up, but your line protocol is down, this is probably the setting you need to change. See Chapter 4 for the common encapsulation types.

Configuring Interfaces

You enter configuration information for a single interface in configure mode (as discussed in Chapter 2), but to do so you must specify the interface that configuration applies to. After you're in configuration mode, enter the interface name.

```
router#conf t
router(config)#int faste2/0
router(❶config-if)#
```

The ❶ config-if (Cisco-ese for "configure interface") label indicates that configuration changes you make will only apply to the single interface you specified.

To leave either interface configuration mode or router configuration mode, enter CTRL-Z.

Ethernet Interfaces

Almost every Cisco router has one or more Ethernet interfaces. Ethernet is a broadcast medium. Many devices can be attached to a single Ethernet network, and information transmitted by a host is broadcast across the entire Ethernet network. Almost all modern office networks are Ethernet.

Theoretically, every host on an Ethernet network sees all data transmitted by every host on that Ethernet. (While switches mostly direct broadcasts to only the destination computer, even a top-of-the-line switch still "leaks" some information to all the hosts on the network.) If you're having trouble with your local Ethernet, a bad switch is the most common cause. (If you're still using a hub, that's almost certainly the problem. Please join the 21st century at your earliest opportunity.) Be sure to check hubs and switches before you blame your router.

While Ethernet has been run over a wide variety of physical media in the past, today almost everyone uses either category 5 cable or some sort of fiber. (You may well find an antediluvian Cisco 2500 with an AUI port, but most of those will also have a 10BaseT Ethernet port.)

From the Cisco point of view, all Ethernet interfaces are configured the same way; just remember that the connection speed will only be as fast as the slowest network device. For example, if you plug a 100Mb Ethernet switch into a 10Mb Ethernet router, the connection will be limited to 10Mb.

Here is the beginning of the output from a sho int on a typical Cisco Fast Ethernet interface. Let's look at some of the useful Ethernet-specific information.

```
router#sho int faste2/0
FastEthernet2/0 is up, line protocol is up
  Hardware is AmdFE, address is ❶0003.e35e.d1a1 (❷bia 0003.e35e.d1a1)
...
  Keepalive set (10 sec)
  ❸Half-duplex, ❹10Mb/s, ❺100BaseTX/FX
  ARP type: ARPA, ARP Timeout 04:00:00
...
```

The first interesting thing is the ❶ MAC (Media Access Control) address, or Ethernet address, 0003.e35e.d1a1. This is a 48-bit number that is, in theory, unique to each Ethernet device. (In practice, some vendors reuse Ethernet addresses, because the chances of two devices with the same MAC address winding up on the same network are negligible.) Because Cisco routers allow you to change the MAC address of an Ethernet interface, they also show the ❷ original burned-in address (bia) assigned to the device by the manufacturer in parentheses. The MAC address and bia address match in this case.

Active Ethernet interfaces also show the ❸ duplex setting, which is half-duplex in this case. (The duplex is usually automatically negotiated between the router and the switch it's attached to.)

Don't worry about configuring autonegotiation, as that takes place in the hardware and cannot be configured. You can hard-code this setting, but doing so can cause all sorts of trouble if you change equipment or if the connected switch has problems. While your switch might support 100Mb/s full duplex today, if it has a problem and must fall back to half-duplex, your hard-coded duplex setting will bring the circuit down. It's better to stay up in a degraded mode than to go down entirely! Your best bet, if possible, is to allow your router to autonegotiate its duplex setting unless you already understand the issues involved.

An active interface also shows the current ❹ network speed. Again, while you can hard-code this, it is generally best to let the router negotiate with the switch or hub it is connected to in order to learn what speeds it can best support. Finally, you can see the ❺ type of physical medium connected to this interface. As you can see, this high-quality fast Ethernet interface is connected to a slow, half-duplex, 10MB network device.

Configuring Ethernet Interfaces

The only change you must make to an Ethernet interface to get it on the network is to give it an IP address.

```
router(config-if)#ip address <ip address> <netmask>
```

In most small network environments, the Ethernet interface's IP address is the default gateway of the attached network. For example, to set the IP address to 192.168.1.1, with a netmask of 255.255.255.128, you would use the following command.

```
router(config-if)#ip address 192.168.1.1 255.255.255.128
```

After you have this basic configuration, you can go on to a variety of other settings.

Description

While entering a description is almost pointless for a simple router with a single T1 port and a single Ethernet, the description field is very useful when your router has multiple Ethernet interfaces. Enter a description with the description keyword.

```
router(config-if)#description DMZ network
```

duplex

By default, the router will attempt to autonegotiate the duplex setting of a connection. You can force a particular setting with the duplex keyword, which has three legitimate settings: auto, half, and full. Here, we force a connection into half-duplex mode. (You might try this if the router negotiates a full-duplex connection but seems to be dropping packets.)

```
router(config-if)#duplex half
```

Cisco recommends leaving duplex at the default setting (auto) so the router will negotiate its own best duplex.

speed

Much like duplex settings, the router will attempt to negotiate the best possible network bandwidth with its switch or hub. You can make the router run at only a single bandwidth setting and refuse to run at other speeds with the speed setting.

Legitimate values for the speed setting vary widely with the interface type, but you can ask an interface what speeds it supports with the standard ? syntax. Here we interrogate an interface to determine supported speeds and then hard-code a desired speed into the configuration.

```
router(config-if)#speed ?
  10    Force 10 Mbps operation
  100   Force 100 Mbps operation
  auto  Enable AUTO speed configuration
router(config-if)#speed 100
```

The problem with hard-coding speed is that if you change your hub or switch without changing the router setting, your Ethernet interface may either stop working or perform suboptimally. Much like the duplex setting, if you hard-code a speed, your router will refuse to fall back to a degraded mode. There's nothing quite like tracing a troublesome network issue down to an obsolete hard-coded network speed; it makes me ask, "Who was the idiot who set this?"[1] I recommend leaving duplex on auto, the default.

Disabling Broadcast Pings

The IP top address in every network (the address ending in .255 for a network with a 255.255.255.0 netmask) is the broadcast address. Traditionally, a ping to that address makes every machine on that network respond. While this was useful for troubleshooting and maintenance, network attackers discovered that they could use this to create one of the first distributed denial-of-service (DDoS) attacks. Today, it's generally considered wise to disable your router's ability to relay these directed broadcast pings from the local network.

```
router(config-if)#no ip directed-broadcast
```

Multicast Routing Cache

By default, modern Cisco IOS versions enable a routing cache for multicast networking, which would improve performance

---

[1] The answer to this question is usually "me."

for multicast routing operation. However, they then disable this cache in the default configuration. (I'm sure they have a good reason for not just disabling it by default, really.) This shows up in your configuration as no ip mroute-cache. If you are using multicast routing, get rid of this configuration statement.

```
router(config-if)#ip mroute-cache
```

Interface Media Type

Older routers (such as some frequently found on auction sites) have both an AUI and a 10BaseT Ethernet port. Despite appearances, these routers have only one Ethernet interface with only two connectors. You can use either the AUI port or the 10BaseT port, but not both simultaneously. Choose the connector you want with the media-type keyword and either the aui or 10baseT setting.

```
router(config-if)#media-type 10baseT
```

This is unnecessary on routers with a single physical plug per Ethernet interface. You can identify these routers easily enough by looking at the Ethernet ports.

Serial Interfaces

A serial network has only two nodes, one at each end, and only transmits data between those two points. This makes managing a serial link much simpler than an Ethernet one, but the line connecting your router to the remote network has a far wider variety of options that can be set.

While you can run a serial link between two routers by attaching the right cable between their serial ports, a serial line is usually provided by a phone company and runs between two different locations much farther apart than the few hundred feet that Ethernet can tolerate. We'll concentrate on telco-provided T1 circuits like the ones you would find in an ISP connection or between two offices.

Here's the beginning of the sho int output of a typical Cisco T1 interface. Despite the scary reputation serial interfaces have, a serial line is in many ways much simpler to configure than an Ethernet interface, because it has many fewer options.

```
Serial1/0 is up, line protocol is up
❶Hardware is DSCC4 with integrated T1 CSU/DSU
...
```

❷Encapsulation PPP, loopback not set

...

First, we see information about the ❶ hardware in this interface. While nobody without a great deal of Cisco experience has any clue what a DSCC4 is, the integrated T1 CSU/DSU hints that this is a T1 line. (If you don't know what a CSU/DSU is, see "Circuit Design" in Chapter 5.)

Further down, we see the ❷ encapsulation field. The encapsulation is the physical protocol spoken by the routers on both ends of the line, just as we discussed earlier. The two common choices for T1 lines are Point-to-Point Protocol (PPP) and High-level Data Link Control (HDLC). PPP (the protocol used in this example) is an old standard spoken by many different routers and modems, while HDLC is a Cisco-created protocol designed especially for high-bandwidth lines. While HDLC is more efficient than PPP, either works well for circuits of T1 size or smaller. The important thing to remember is that the routers on both sides of the circuit must use the same physical protocol on a circuit. If one router claims that a circuit is speaking PPP, while the other insists that it's HDLC, the line protocol will go down and stay down until the misconfiguration is fixed.

Configuring Serial Interfaces

The two basic things to configure on a serial interface are the IP address and the encapsulation. For example, suppose we have a T1 with an IP address of 192.168.1.2, a netmask of 255.255.255.252, and PPP encapsulation. Go into configure mode for that interface and enter

```
router(config-if)#ip address 192.168.1.2 255.255.255.252
router(config-if)#encapsulation ppp
```

NOTE   *We cover configuring serial interfaces in greater detail in Chapter 4. Refer to Cisco's online documentation for more details.*

Modern Cisco routers set a variety of configurations by default, most of which disable functionality that is only used in advanced implementations. One setting that is worth changing, though, is the interface description, a field that can be a useful way to store important circuit-related information. Here we label our Internet circuit as such, to differentiate it from our other T1 circuits, and we include the circuit ID that the telephone company uses to identify this particular T1 circuit. This way, if we should have to phone the telco and complain that a circuit is down, we have the necessary circuit ID right at hand.

```
router(config-if)#description ISP uplink, circuit ID#3141579
```

Other Interfaces

Cisco supports a whole slew of different interface types: HSSI, FDDI, SMDS, and ATM, to name a few. If you need one of these interfaces, the interface card or router will come with documentation describing how the interface is configured. Chances are good that the configuration process will closely resemble the one used for serial or Ethernet circuits, with minor changes for the connection protocol. Because these interfaces are comparatively rare among the people likely to read this book, we're not going to cover them in any detail.

However, every router has two other sorts of interfaces that we will address: loopback and null interfaces. Both are logical interfaces—they have no hardware associated with them, but are created purely in software for the router to handle certain specialized tasks. Each has its own specific uses.

Loopback Interfaces

Loopback interfaces are ones where the local router communicates with itself. They are useful because you can assign any IP address you like to them. For example, some advanced router configurations require the router to have its own IP address without assigning that IP to any interface attached to the network. Loopback interfaces make this easy.

You create loopback interfaces by configuring them. For example, to create an interface called loopback0, you would go into configure mode and tell the router you're configuring that interface, then assign it an IP address as with any other interface.

```
router# conf t
router(config) int loopback0
router(config-if)#ip address 192.168.254.5 netmask
255.255.255.255
router(config-ip)#^Z
```

The next time you run sho int, the loopback interface you created appears in the list. Our router now knows that the IP address 192.168.254.5 is bound to this router, but not to any particular interface. If someone attempts to ping that IP over any interface, the router will respond.

To remove the loopback interface, go into configure mode and enter **no** and the interface name.

```
router#conf t
router(config)#no int loopback0
```

These interfaces are especially useful when combining two or more circuits into one large one with multilink PPP, and then using BGP (see Chapter 7) over such a link. You need to have a single IP address for a BGP peer, but when you share several circuits between you and your BGP peer, you need to have a consistent IP address for those peers to talk to. You should never create a loopback interface unless specifically instructed to by your ISP or by Cisco's tech support, but on a similar note, you should know what they are so that they don't surprise you.

Null Interfaces

The null interface is quite literally a route to nowhere. Traffic routed to any null interface is simply discarded. Why would you want to discard traffic? Some IP addresses should never be seen on the public Internet, and you might wish to route those addresses to the bottomless void if packets arrive for them. Null interfaces are most commonly used in BGP configurations, where you must have a static route for each block you wish to announce. (We'll discuss BGP in more detail in Chapter 7.)

Only one null interface is required, null0; having multiple black holes in your router doesn't serve any purpose. The null interface doesn't need to be configured; you can simply route traffic to it.

```
router(config-ip)#ip route 192.168.0.0 255.255.0.0 null0
```

Now that we've explored the basics of router interfaces, let's see how to use serial interfaces in the real world.

4

WIDE AREA NETWORK CONNECTIONS

Cisco excels in wide area networks (WANs), connecting different sites over telephone company circuits. To many people, a T1 or DS3 connection is some mysterious "thing" that provides the Internet or connects corporate offices to headquarters. Once you know a little about them, however, network circuits are far less mysterious than whatever makes the boss's computer crash three times a day.

Wide area networks are mainly used for connections to the Internet via an ISP, or for connecting two offices over a private network. We'll discuss both uses.

Internet Connections

Chances are good that readers of this book were handed the office Internet connection one day and told, "Here, take care of this." Maybe this inherited Internet connection works flawlessly and silently. However, if you are in the market for a new Internet connection, or if you want to replace the atrocity of a circuit you currently endure, read on. You've got a large variety of ISPs to choose from and a bewildering variety of service packages. It can be difficult to sort them all out, but here are some tips to help you decide.

Choosing an ISP

Choosing an Internet circuit is difficult when compared to, say, buying a car. When you need a car, you have some idea of your needs. You know how many people you have to haul around, how often you need to move large objects, and what sort of comfort features you want, and you can put all this together and make a mostly intelligent decision between the SUV and the subcompact.

To make an informed choice about network bandwidth, you'll need to have the same sort of information. For one thing, you need to determine how much bandwidth your company actually uses. You can get a vague idea from random spot checks of throughput on the serial interface on your router's Internet circuit, but this is haphazard and unreliable.

If you log in once an hour to see how much bandwidth your router is using, you can easily miss random peaks. Your best bet is to use a tool like MRTG (http://www.mrtg.org) to gather statistics on your bandwidth usage over days or weeks. Even if you're not in a decision-making position, knowing how much bandwidth your company uses will help your decision makers and will also make you look good.

No matter how much bandwidth you have, at some time your company will consume all of it. For example, downloading an ISO image from a high-bandwidth site can soak up an entire T1 for several minutes and smaller circuits for proportionately longer.

But consider this: How often do you use all of your bandwidth, and how urgent are those high-volume requests? When you do need to download an entire ISO, do you need it in ten minutes or would an hour suffice? In my experience working for ISPs, most companies that purchase a T1 use less than a tenth of their bandwidth 99 percent of the time. If you *know* that 128Kb/second would more than meet your company's needs, you will be completely justified in laughing when a sales person attempts to sell you three bonded T1s with live failover for 4.5Mb/second of high-quality throughput. It sounds great, but you probably don't need it.

When you know what you need, you can easily gather a list of providers in your area from any search engine. Make a list of those who provide the service you require, and then start weeding them out. Talk to network staff at other companies and ask who they get Internet service through and how satisfied they are. Look for complaints in public newsgroups and websites; while every company has a few dissatisfied customers, do the number of complaints about any one company seem excessive compared to the others? See what you think. After you've weeded out the obvious losers from your list, you can probably group the remainder into four categories:

Big telcos These are companies like SBC and Pacific Bell Internet, who have Big Names and correspondingly Big Prices. They frequently offer high levels of service, because they own the phone circuit as well as the Internet service. These companies can be difficult to work with when things go wrong, however, especially for small customers. Getting unusual problems resolved can take quite some time.

National ISPs These are big Internet companies such as Level3 and Verio. Many times, these companies have unadvertised links to a big telco. For example, as of this writing Verio is owned by the Japanese telephone company NTT. Because they are pure Internet companies, they frequently have a better understanding of the Internet's unique requirements and technologies than telco-based ISPs. These companies will frequently carry your traffic across the country to get it to someone on the other side of town, simply because that's their closest connection to the other person's provider.

Regional ISPs These are local companies that cover a city, a state, or a few states. While they are generally clients of the telcos and national ISPs, they have a variety of connections in a variety of locations to a variety of providers. Some of these companies have excellent customer service, while others have service that is not so good. Regional ISPs are frequently more flexible than larger ones and have the technical staff to back it up.

Mom-and-pop ISPs   It's perfectly feasible for someone to set up a medium-sized router in his basement and start selling T1s. These companies can be inexpensive and fairly reliable; because the mom-and-pop ISP doesn't have a huge number of customers, it cares about each and every one it has. Frequently, these ISPs are underfunded and under-equipped, which can be a risk, but their prices are good, and they usually don't flinch from special requests.

Having been employed by all four types, I have to say that my favorite is a good regional ISP. Your experiences in your area may vary.

ISP Router Configuration

Your ISP should help configure your router or at least provide a configuration for the interface connecting to them. For the most part, you can accept what they give you; they're in the business of hooking customers up to the Internet every day, and you're in the business of hooking up this solitary T1 as soon as possible. If you're going to build a configuration by hand, however, ask for this information:

Serial interface IP addresses   Most ISPs give each end of a T1 an IP address and assign a block of four IP addresses (with a netmask of 255.255.255.252) to the circuit network. The bottom and top IP addresses in this block are not usable; one of the remaining addresses is assigned to each end of the circuit. You must know which IP goes on each end in order to configure your router appropriately. While you can use a serial line without an IP address, doing so will make troubleshooting and sophisticated routing more difficult.

Circuit ID or customer number   If you should have a T1 failure, you will need to contact the ISP in a hurry. If possible, get the circuit ID for this circuit and/or your ISP's customer number for your company so that you have this information handy when you call.

T1 line encapsulation   You must set the encapsulation on your circuit. Common choices are HDLC and PPP (discussed in Chapter 3). As long as both your router and your ISP's router use the same encapsulation protocol, the circuit will work.

Ethernet IP addresses   Every client of an ISP should get a block of IP addresses for machines on their network. Usually, these addresses are assigned to firewalls, desktop machines, or other computers. With the prevalence of Network Address Translation (NAT) and proxy firewalls, this block may be as small as eight IP addresses. Your job is to decide which address in the block will be assigned to your router's Ethernet interface (usually the first or last usable address in the block).

As soon as you have this information, you can configure your router to connect to your ISP. Your first step is to log in to the router and enter configure mode.

We discussed each of the following entries in Chapter 3, but basically, by setting an IP address and an encapsulation proto- col, you should bring your circuit up.

```
router#conf t
router(config)#int <serial interface name>
router(config-if)#description ISP Uplink, circuit ID #<circuit
ID>, customer #<number>
router(config-if)#encapsulation <encapsulation>
router(config-if)ip address <your end of circuit IP address>
<netmask>
router(config-if)^Z
```

After you enter the above commands, your T1 should show a status and line protocol of "up." Ping the ISP's side of the T1 line, and you should get a response. Once you do, you know that your T1 is up. *Save your work immediately!*

```
router#write memory

Building configuration...
[OK]
```

Now configure the router's Ethernet interface.

```
router#conf t
router(config)#int <Ethernet interface name>
router(config-if)ip address <IP address for router> <netmask>
router(config-if)^Z
```

Although you can add any other Ethernet configuration infor- mation you like, such as hard-coding duplex, I suggest that you start with the simplest possible configuration. When you have this configuration set, you should be able to ping any host on your local LAN. (Again, as soon as this interface is configured, save your work!)

Finally, set the router's default route. This is where the router will send any packets that need to reach the Internet and should be the IP address of the ISP's side of the T1.

```
router(config)#ip route 0.0.0.0 0.0.0.0 <ISP side of T1 circuit>
```

With this route in place, you should be able to ping any host on the public Internet.

Some ISPs will have special configuration requirements for their circuits, which they should be able to give you and then walk you through configuring your circuit. If you are bringing up a big circuit such as a DS3 or OC-48, you'll need a slightly more advanced setup. However, these settings will be dictated by the ones chosen by your ISP, so ask them. ISP technicians are usually happy to answer these sorts of questions, as setting things correctly in the beginning will prevent problems later.

That's not that hard, is it? Building a private connection isn't much more difficult.

Private Connections

Another popular use for routers is connecting two offices together with a private T1, using a virtual private network (VPN). While VPNs are increasing in popularity, they cannot provide the broad, dedicated interoffice bandwidth that many companies require. A VPN adds additional overhead to the traffic between offices and also increases the circuit utilization. If you're editing a document on a workstation on one side of the VPN, and someone else in the office starts downloading an ISO image from the Internet, your access to the document server may slow to the point of being unbearable. A dedicated connection, on the other hand, doesn't fight for the same resources as your Internet connection.

Figure 4-1 shows a typical private T1 setup at most companies. In most cases, this consists of a T1 at the main office and T1s radiating from the main office to the branch offices. (Of course, the main office usually also has the firewalls, mail servers, and other paraphernalia required to keep a company on the Internet, but we'll ignore this clutter for our purposes and concentrate on just the Cisco routers.) Headquarters will also typically have a second router for branch-office connections, with the branch office network behind it and a router at each branch office that handles the T1 to headquarters.

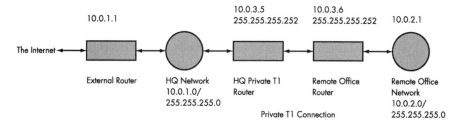

Figure 4-1: A typical private T1 setup

All Internet access is handled by the external Internet router. The headquarters network supports the staff at the main office. To support the private T1 connection to the remote office we have two routers, one at the HQ office and one at the remote office. Finally, at the remote office we have the remote office network to support those users.

This setup has several advantages. First, all user and system administration is handled by staff on the HQ network, while users at the remote office can access all network services at the main office far more quickly than they could over a VPN. Second, with proper software running on the remote office's desktop computers, such as VNC[1] or Windows Terminal Services, the main office can perform all support as well, and the remote office can piggyback on the main office's Internet access.

The only catch is that someone has to configure all of this. The good news is that it won't be too tough to get this all up and running with what you know already. Once you have management buy-in to the idea, here's a basic overview of what you'll need to do to set up a private network:

1. Choose equipment for both ends.
2. Order circuits and equipment.
3. Configure the routers.
4. Install the routers and circuits.

We'll discuss each step in turn.

---

[1] VNC, or Virtual Network Computing, is a really nifty cross-platform system for remote GUI-based computer administration. And it's free. If you support older versions of Windows that don't have Terminal Services, or if you have a variety of platforms and want to standardize on a single management tool, investigate VNC.

Choosing Equipment

Perhaps the biggest up-front expense is purchasing the router. Your ISP might have a recommended model, and you should let yourself by guided by their experience. If you need to choose a router, Cisco makes a wide variety of small T1 office routers, and even their smallest T1-capable router will probably be more than sufficient for your needs.

If you have multiple branch offices and are considering implementing private T1s between offices, a larger, multi-interface router for headquarters might tempt you, but I still recommend purchasing the smallest router available with enough interfaces. I won't recommend any particular model here, because by the time this book is actually printed, it will have changed. Whatever you buy, be sure to get SmartNet support with the model you choose, and be certain to remind your financial people that the support must be renewed every year. Support will quickly become indispensable once you install that private circuit, and the business cost of an extra hour of downtime will far exceed the cost of the support contract.

NOTE   *You can always pick up a used router on eBay (http://www.ebay.com) and at other used equipment sites. But before you purchase, check Cisco's website to be sure that the model you're considering is still supported. It's easy to get an old Cisco 2500 router that can support a T1, but you will be completely on your own if it breaks! Also, Cisco will frequently require that you purchase an additional software agreement for this used equipment, even if it's still under warranty. Their view is that while a customer can resell the hardware, they do not have the right to resell the software that runs on it. While many people consider this ridiculous, Cisco takes their claims very seriously, and because they're the only people who can provide support for your equipment, you should take them seriously as well.*

Ordering Circuits

After you've got your equipment, you need to order a circuit, which can be intimidating if you haven't provisioned one before. Unless you can pick up a roll of wire and string it through trees, along fences, and over the freeways all the way to your remote office, you'll have to deal with a telephone company. If you are one of the few with this expertise, you'll agree that it's almost always a better idea to order through the telco anyway. (Much like ISPs, T1 circuit providers vary widely from area to area. Consult with your local user groups and other network administrators to see who delivers good service in your area.)

When ordering your circuit, remember that most private circuits are priced per mile, which means that it will be much less expensive to connect offices 20 miles apart than it will be to connect offices 200 miles apart! Note also that private circuits are not suitable for distances of more than a few hundred miles.

NOTE *For longer distances, you should probably use a less expensive technology, like frame relay. While we won't cover frame relay configuration in this book, Cisco's frame-relay documentation should suffice to get you up and running.*

Who Installs the Circuit?

Many people do not realize that the circuit you will end up with will probably be installed by a single company, regardless of who you purchase it through: generally a Regional Bell Operating Company (RBOC) or its descendant. For example, in much of my area of the United States (the Midwest), all circuits are delivered to the customer by SBC. If I order a circuit through a different company, an SBC technician will show up at my office to install it. Even though you purchase your circuit from a vendor other than your RBOC, that vendor must turn around and purchase the installation from the RBOC.

Because the level of service that the RBOC provides to independent telcos is regulated by the federal government, many independent telcos can provide better service than you will get by dealing directly with the RBOC. The downside to this system is that if the circuit breaks, you generally have to call your vendor to get them to call the RBOC to get the circuit fixed. This creates additional distance between you and anyone who can actually fix the problem, and can be quite frustrating during a crisis. On the other hand, a third-party vendor can frequently leverage these regulations to get a circuit delivered more quickly than you could get it if you placed the order directly with the RBOC.

When you finally call to place your order, all you'll need is a landline phone number at each of the two locations. The phone company knows exactly where these phones are and will be able to give you a quote on a circuit between those locations.

Data or Voice Circuit?

Most telcos today are very well acquainted with private data circuits—in fact, some salespeople have never sold anything but data circuits! Telcos provide a whole variety of circuits, however, so be certain to specify that you want a data circuit when ordering. While a voice circuit might work for a modem, it certainly won't work as a dedicated data circuit.

When the purchase order arrives, confirm that you're getting a data circuit (most are encoded as "B8ZS"). If your order form does not specify a data circuit or state that it has B8ZS encoding, review the paperwork with your salesperson. If your paperwork states that the circuit has "AMI" encoding, it's flat-out wrong, and you need to have a pointed conversation with your telco representative.

In most parts of the United States, delivery time for a T1 circuit will be two to four weeks (or as specified on your completed order form). Be certain to get a real delivery date from your vendor, however; if the RBOC has to dig a trench across the road to deliver your T1, it will take a little longer.

NOTE   *If you're not in the United States, you'll want to investigate your country's telephone system before attempting to place an order. Much as if you were shopping for an ISP, talk to other network administrators to see what sort of service your different possible vendors offer. In many countries with a telco monopoly, service is slow at best. Plan ahead.*

Private Circuit Configuration

While your circuit is on order, you can preconfigure your router. Configuring a Cisco router for a private connection is almost exactly the same as configuring it for an ISP connection. As long as the configuration of the router on each end is consistent, there's really very little you can do to mess it up. In most situations, the hardest part of the configuration process is choosing the IP addresses for your circuit.

Private Circuit IP Addresses

You'll need IP addresses for both ends of your T1 circuit and for at least one Ethernet interface on each router. To number the Ethernet interface, just pick an IP address on the local LAN. Every device in the remote office will use the IP address of the remote office router's Ethernet as the default gateway. At headquarters, the IP address of the router connecting the remote office is also the route to the remote office.

While private circuits don't strictly require IP addresses (you could always use "unnumbered" interfaces), troubleshooting is much simpler when each side of the circuit has an IP, because then you can ping either side of a circuit and get a response that you know is from the circuit interface. Numbering IP addresses also makes it much easier to sort out your interfaces when performing network monitoring. I strongly recommend numbering interfaces whenever possible—and it's almost always possible.

Reserved Addresses

Several blocks of IP addresses are reserved for use on private networks. If you're using NAT (Network Address Translation), chances are good that you're already familiar with them. The address blocks are:

10.0.0.0 through 10.255.255.255

172.16.0.0 through 172.31.255.255

192.168.0.0 through 192.168.255.255

If your internal network falls into any of these ranges, you're already using private IP addresses. If not, you can use any of these blocks to number your private network interfaces. (You could also use actual IP addresses assigned to your company to make those private circuits accessible to the outside world, but that's usually neither necessary nor desirable.)

Subnetting

Each circuit requires two IP addresses in a legitimate subnet. Remember, in any block of IP addresses, the highest and lowest addresses are not usable,[2] so we need a network of four IP addresses.

NOTE *If you're not familiar with netmasks other than 255.255.255.0, or if you've never seen subnets labeled with suffixes such as /30, be sure to read the appendix for a full explanation before continuing. You must understand subnetting before you can properly assign addresses or perform advanced routing.*

Each usable subnet of four IP addresses has a first number evenly divisible by 4. For example, 10.0.3.0 through 10.0.3.3 is a usable block (0 is evenly divisible by 4), as is 10.0.3.28 through

---

[2] On those rare occasions when you have both time *and* a network to kill, assign a system (on an average 255.255.255.0-netmask LAN) an IP address ending in .0 or .255 and see what happens. Something will break, but you might not figure out what it was for some time.

10.0.3.31 (28 is also evenly divisible by 4). However, 10.0.3.207 through 10.0.3.210 is not usable because 207 is not evenly divisible by 4.

Because some (increasingly rare) network devices have trouble with the first and last subnet in a block, I recommend starting with the fifth through eighth addresses in a block and working up. Because we're beginning our count from 0, this would be .4 through .7. (If any of this confuses you, even a little bit, go read the appendix.)

So, if you're using 10.0.1.0/255.255.255.0 as your headquarters LAN IP addresses, and 10.0.2.0/255.255.255.0 as your remote office IP addresses, you might decide to carve up 10.0.3.0 for router interfaces. In this example, we'll use the addresses 10.0.3.4 through 10.0.3.7. However, because 10.0.3.4 and 10.0.3.7 are not usable (because they are the first and last IP addresses in the block), we'll assign 10.0.3.5 to the headquarters side of our circuit and 10.0.3.6 to the remote office.

With this information, you can configure both routers. On your main office router, enter configure mode and give the interface its IP address. Here, we configure the interface "serial1" with the IP address 10.0.3.5 and assign it the proper netmask for a block of four IPs. This should look exceedingly familiar from our recent adventures configuring Internet T1s.

```
router#conf t
router(config)#int s1
router(config-if)#ip address 10.0.3.5 255.255.255.252
```

Now exit configure mode and save your work. Your interface should simply come up when you plug in the circuit (especially if your routers are identical models running the same version of the IOS).

If the circuit doesn't come up, do a sho int on both routers and compare the configurations. The interfaces should have identical setups; if they don't, make them match by changing the configuration (as discussed in Chapter 3).

The most common misconfiguration between peer routers is the default line encapsulation: make sure that they're both set to either PPP or HDLC. (HDLC is generally preferable on broadband circuits.) A mismatch of default encapsulation is especially likely if you are using different router models.

When you have your serial lines up, configure an IP address on your Ethernet interface. These are configured exactly as they would be for a standard Internet connection; just assign an IP address and a netmask, and they should come right up.

Routing Configuration

Now that you have a circuit set up between offices, it's time to figure out how to guide traffic to its destination. Remember that each desktop machine at headquarters has a default route telling it to send all traffic to the main (external) router, so if that router cannot send traffic to the remote office, all this is for nothing. The purpose of *routing* is to tell routers where to send packets that belong to particular networks of IP addresses.

You can fire up RIP or some other dynamic routing protocol to guide your traffic around the network, but doing so has a lot of disadvantages. Dynamic protocols break, increase non-useful network traffic, and may pose security risks.

Static Routing

On a simple network, it's much better to simply attach static routes to various sections of the network and have all traffic flow in a deterministic manner. In the long run, this method is much more maintainable and causes fewer problems on a network like this. (If you have several internal circuits with multiple routes between different locations, consider using a dynamic routing protocol.[3])

The syntax for a static route statement is:

```
router(config)#ip route ❶destination-ip-network ❷netmask ❸gateway
```

The ❶ destination IP address is the first IP in the network block. The ❷ netmask is the netmask of the destination netblock. (Remember, when you route, you route entire blocks of addresses, not individual IPs.)

Finally, the ❸ gateway is an IP address that is the next hop where packets for this block should be sent. This gateway should be an IP address that the router knows how to reach but is not on the router itself. On most routers, this will be the IP address on the far side of a serial link. For example, if we wanted to provide a static route to the IP address block 100.100.50.0, netmask 255.255.254.0, through the gateway of 10.0.3.5, we would use the following command.

```
router(config)#ip route 100.100.50.0 255.255.254.0 10.0.3.5
```

---

[3] Even in this case, I can't recommend any sort of RIP. Investigate OSPF instead.

NOTE *One thing to remember about routing (on almost any system, not just Cisco) is that the most specific route for a particular IP address is taken. For example, almost every router has a "default route" where it sends packets bound for another network. If you have a more specific route for certain IP addresses, that more specific route will be taken instead of the default. We'll see some examples of this later.*

As you saw in Figure 4-1, all traffic on the remote office LAN is either local or routed through the T1 to headquarters. In the main office, all traffic that is not destined specifically for the remote office is either local or goes to the exterior router. This design is simple and doesn't resort to error-prone dynamic routing protocols.

Remote Office Routing

In this scenario, every host on the remote office network needs a default route that points to the IP address of the remote office router's Ethernet interface. This is best done on the DHCP server. The router then needs to know to send outbound traffic to the far side of the serial line.

Because all traffic on the remote office LAN needs to go to the headquarters router, you only need a single route statement.

```
router#conf t
router(config)#ip route ❶0.0.0.0 ❷0.0.0.0 ❸10.0.3.5
```

The ❶ first 0.0.0.0 is our destination IP address, and the ❷ second 0.0.0.0 is the netmask. This combination means "every IP address in the world." The router knows that the IP addresses in the 10.0.2.0 network block are attached to a local interface, so it will not send those packets across the WAN. Lastly, the ❸ gateway IP address is the IP address of the headquarters side of the T1 (in this case).

Headquarters Routing

Our headquarters' private T1 router has a slightly more complicated configuration. It must know that traffic bound for the remote office must be sent across the private T1, but all other traffic should go to the exterior router's Ethernet interface at 10.0.1.1.

```
router(config)# ip route ❶10.0.2.0 255.255.255.0 ❷10.0.3.6
router(config)# ip route ❸0.0.0.0 0.0.0.0 ❹10.0.1.1
```

In this configuration, we first send the ❶ specific network block used in the remote office to the ❷ far side of the private T1. Then we add the ❸ default route to send all other traffic to the exterior router's Ethernet interface. (In practice, you can add these routes in either order and the router will put them in the order it prefers.) The route for the 10.0.2.0 network block is more specific than the default route, so that route is preferred over the default route for those IP addresses.

The external router should already have a default route pointing to the outside world, but it must know where to send traffic for both the remote office *and* for the serial link addresses.

```
router(config)# ip route ❶10.0.2.0 255.255.255.0 ❷10.0.1.2
router(config)# ip route ❸10.0.3.4 ❹255.255.255.252 ❺10.0.1.2
```

Just like on our private T1 router at headquarters, we route the ❶ 10.0.2.0 block further into the network—but this time, to the ❷ IP address of the private line router's Ethernet interface. We then route the ❸ IP addresses used on the private T1 to the ❺ same Ethernet interface.

NOTE *We specify ❹ the netmask for the private line's IP addresses; if you add another private circuit to a second field office, you'll want to route the IPs for that circuit to its router separately.*

Plugging It All Together

After the router is configured, you wouldn't think that actually plugging everything together would be a problem, would you? It will probably work just fine, but let's go through what you can do when things go wrong.

First, make sure that you use a good-quality Cat 5 cable to connect your CSU/DSU or router to the smartjack. You can get away with the cheap stuff on the secretary's Ethernet connection, but telco circuits are sensitive. Use a cable of the correct length; don't coil up the surplus and leave it dangling from the wall, and don't stretch it taut like a tripwire. Cable quality is responsible for a fair number of problems.

In theory, after the circuit is plugged into your preconfigured router, you should be able to activate the routers at each end, and the circuit should just come up. At this point, log in to the routers and make sure that your serial line has a status of "up" and a line protocol of "up." If the line is up, but the protocol is down, double-check your line encapsulation and then the rest of your configuration.

If you've confirmed that the interfaces are correctly configured, but the line still doesn't come up, phone the company that sold you the circuit and have them test it. If the telco can successfully and cleanly loop up the CSU/DSU at both ends, and your configuration is correct, your hardware is bad. Contact Cisco and get the help you need; new parts can be on site in as little as four hours.

Now that your circuit is up, it should stay that way. But let's look at what happens when it doesn't.

5

TROUBLESHOOTING ROUTERS

Now that you have a basic understanding of how the router is configured and how the various network types work, let's consider the most common day-to-day router problems. These can be boiled down into two groups:

- Router crashes
- Network failure or slowness

By following a few straightforward steps, you'll have a reasonable chance of fixing many of these problems. In the worst case, you can at least be well armed with diagnostic information when you call your ISP.

Router Crashes

For the most part, Cisco routers keep working. On rare occasions, an untouched router will intermittently reboot itself, or just shut itself off when it feels like it. In these situations, a SmartNet contract is invaluable—Cisco devices are mostly black boxes, and if something goes wrong with one, the warranty may be your only recourse. Still, there are a few things you can do to try to resolve the problem without a service contract.

A crashing router will often print errors to the serial console. Attach the serial console to the router and leave it there. Any crash messages will remain in the serial terminal's message buffer. Copy the messages exactly, and search on them in Google or http://www.cisco.com; you may well identify the problem. Cisco's technical support will certainly want to know what these messages say.

If you cannot discover the problem through the crash messages, check the hardware itself; perhaps something's come loose inside the router. Open the case and remove any dust that has worked its way in, preferably with compressed air. Reseat every removable component, such as memory or flash cards, as well as add-on modules such as Cisco WIC cards and port adapters. When you are certain that everything is tightly attached, replace the router in the rack and turn it on. If you're lucky, it will work.

NOTE *Cisco offers articles on how to diagnose router crashes for various models; some articles are accessible without a SmartNet contract. It's always worth searching http://www.cisco.com for help.*

If your router still crashes, you have no choice but to contact Cisco. (Well, all right, you could choose to live with the problem. A few moments of lost connectivity isn't the worst thing that could happen to a company, but it could hurt your job and definitely interfere with your Internet radio listening.) If you don't have a SmartNet contract, Cisco's technical support will happily transfer you to the sales department or direct you to a reseller.

Network Failure

Network failure is by far the most common router problem, even though, technically, the router itself hasn't failed—the circuit has. Backhoes digging in the wrong spot cause any number of circuit outages (and you'll never fix those yourself).

Before you blame the telco or ISP, however, you can do several things to rule out problems on your end and maybe even quickly fix the problem without outside help.

Most network administrators are fairly skilled at troubleshooting Ethernet problems. Is there a link light? Did the duplex setting change? Is the switch port bad, or did someone trip on the cable and break the little plastic thingamajig on the end? The time-honored magic of replacing cables and switching ports solves most Ethernet problems. Internet circuit failures, on the other hand, are far more difficult to troubleshoot, as you only have a small window into the circuit, and most of it is handled by the ISP or telco.

As with all troubleshooting, the first question to ask yourself is, "Did *I* change anything?" If you made a change and the network went away, try undoing that change to see if the network returns. If that doesn't work, log in to the router and look at the interface of the failed network connection.

Initial Circuit Tests

A phone call from a user screaming, "The Internet is down!" deserves a closer look. But remember, for many users, the Internet is Internet Explorer, or even just Yahoo! (if you're my publisher's mother). I recall one user who insisted the Internet was broken whenever an email took more than five minutes to arrive. Because the email system was badly overloaded, this happened at least three times a week.

If you think that you have an Internet failure, check a variety of network services first. A failure in a nameserver, firewall, proxy server, switch, or other device can appear to be a complete Internet failure to users who depend upon it. The two most helpful diagnostic tests you can perform to determine the extent of an actual Internet circuit outage are ping and traceroute.

Ping

When you ping, you simply send a request to another Internet node asking, "Are you there?" If the remote node receives the request and is not configured to ignore it, it should send a response. A successful ping means that you have basic network connectivity to that node.

When network problems are wide enough that you suspect an Internet circuit failure, your first attempt at resolution should be to log in to your router and try to ping across your

Internet circuit. You may have a domain name for this circuit, but use the IP address, because actual Internet problems also mean DNS problems. Chances are good that the far side of your circuit is the default route on your router. In the following example, the remote side of our serial line has an IP address of 192.168.88.65. Log in to your router and give the ping command and the target IP address.[1]

```
router# ping 192.168.88.65
Type escape sequence to abort.
Sending 5, 100-byte ICMP Echos to 192.168.88.65, timeout is 2 seconds:
❶!!!!!
Success rate is ❷100 percent (5/5), round-trip ❸min/avg/max = 4/4/4 ms
router#
```

The router sends five packets to the destination IP address and gives each two seconds to return. This is generally more than long enough to ping anything that isn't over a satellite link. Each ❶ exclamation point indicates a packet that returns, while a period shows a packet that has vanished. Finally, we see the ❷ success percentages and ❸ some statistics on packet speed, in milliseconds. The circuit shown here is certainly up.

On the other hand, a result like the following indicates your local circuit is down.

```
Sending 5, 100-byte ICMP Echos to 192.168.88.65, timeout is 2 seconds:
❶.....
Success rate is ❷0 percent (0/5)
```

A ❶ period is a dropped packet. Five periods indicate ❷ total circuit failure. Start troubleshooting your circuit!

However, going back to the first ping example, just because your circuit is up doesn't mean that you're on the Internet. Perhaps your ISP had a failure, or some major backbone had a run-in with that rogue backhoe. Your next step is to attempt to reach a popular Internet site such as Yahoo! from your router. If your circuit is passing traffic, but you cannot ping such popular and highly available sites such as Yahoo! or CNN.com, you may have a failure between your network and the main Internet. That's when you use traceroute.

---

[1] It's also possible to try to ping from your desktop computer, but in this case, you're not just testing the router's circuit; you're testing your desktop's connection to the network, any intervening firewalls, and whatever other network equipment lies between your computer and the far side of the circuit. To isolate problems, test only one small piece at a time.

Traceroute

The `traceroute` command sends packets to a remote Internet node and returns the IP address of every node it passes through on the way. Remember that to reach a remote site, your traffic probably travels through your router, your ISP's router, across several backbone routers, through the destination site's ISP's router, and through the destination site's router before reaching the actual target server. If any of these are broken, your request fails.

To use traceroute, just log in to the router and enter the command `traceroute` and the IP address or hostname you're attempting to reach.

```
router#traceroute www.blackhelicopters.org
Translating "www.blackhelicopters.org"...domain server [OK]

Type escape sequence to abort.
Tracing the route to bewilderbeast.blackhelicopters.org (198.22.63.43)

  ❶1 192.150.247.53 [❷AS 26096] ❸4 msec 4 msec 0 msec
  ❹2 192.150.247.38 [AS 26096] 4 msec 8 msec 8 msec
  ❺3 bewilderbeast.blackhelicopters.org (198.22.63.43) [AS 26096] 12 msec
8 msec 8 msec
router#
```

Upon leaving our current router, traffic to the server goes through the router with the IP address of ❶ 192.150.247.53. If this machine had a reverse DNS entry, a hostname would be displayed instead. Of three packets, ❸ two return in four milliseconds, and one returns in zero milliseconds. (This doesn't mean zero time; it just means a smaller time than your router can measure.) This router belongs to the ❷ autonomous system 26096 (see Chapter 7). The ❹ second router is crossed very quickly. On our ❺ third hop, we reach a machine with the reverse DNS of "bewilderbeast.blackhelicopters.org," which is where the traceroute ends. Presumably, the IP address of www.blackhelicopters.org is on this machine.

- When a packet is dropped, you will see an asterisk instead of a timestamp.

- If a traceroute ends in a !H, that means that the last node in the traceroute doesn't know how to reach the destination. This is almost certainly a routing issue.

- Traceroutes are said to "die" when they turn into line after line of three asterisks. This may indicate that a firewall is blocking traceroute packets from reaching the target server, or it could be a network problem. The last node that appears knows where to send the packets, but it is not receiving a response from the next hop.

A traceroute can help you clarify the scope of a problem: if all of your traceroutes reach your ISP's router and die, you can assume that your ISP has a problem and that it's time to give them a call.

If the traceroute dies somewhere out in the middle of the Internet, it's a fair bet that there's nothing you can do, but that the damage is limited in scope. Or there may be some Internet "black hole" that causes many different requests to fail. For example, for much of 1996, MCI's Willow Springs router cluster seemed to be the Secret Internet Packet Burial Ground; network requests routed through that system consistently suffered horrible packet loss and latency. It's highly likely that the owner of such a Network of Death is well aware of the problem and is desperately attempting to resolve the issue, but if you have no business relationship with the network owner, there's nothing you or your ISP can do about it. In either event, at least you know.

If you cannot even ping across your circuit, it's time to get your hands dirty and troubleshoot your circuit. But before you can troubleshoot anything, you must understand it.

Circuit Design

Different phone companies have used many different types of connection equipment over the decades. One of my clients still uses a phone switch dating from the 1950s, featuring fuses the width of my thumb and several inches long. (I believe that Dr. Frankenstein used such equipment, and I have suggested offering the equipment to him for spares if he'll only haul it away.) There is no way this sort of equipment can be used for an Internet connection.

Others have systems of more recent vintage, but of completely unknown origin. If you have such a baroque setup, save yourself a *lot* of trouble and get a modern circuit. We're going to discuss the physical design of a modern T1 circuit, not Frankenstein collectibles.

The Smartjack

Phone companies usually terminate the circuit at your location with a device called a *smartjack*, which is a small box with green and red lights on it. The smartjack has simple brains that the telco can use for troubleshooting (that's where the "smart" part comes from). The phone company or ISP is usually responsible for the circuit up to the smartjack; problems between the smartjack and the router are your responsibility.

The point where the smartjack is installed is called the *demarc*. If your smartjack is far from your router, it's not uncommon to have a professionally installed *extended demarc*, where the circuit is run from the smartjack to a point more convenient for the equipment. You'll frequently see this in office buildings, where the phone company delivers all the circuits to one central location but offices are on many floors above.

Eventually, the circuit is delivered to a Channel Service Unit/Data Service Unit (CSU/DSU), which transforms the signals arriving over the T1 line into something the router understands. Most modern Cisco routers have integrated CSU/DSU features, so you can just plug the RJ-45 cable from the smartjack directly into the router without having additional clunky boxes sitting around the data center.

Examining the Circuit

The first line of the `sho int` output for an interface describes the basic state of the interface, as discussed in Chapter 3. If the line is up, the router is seeing a reasonable signal from the T1. If the line is down, the router is not seeing a signal over the T1. While you still need to check for other errors on the interface, not seeing a signal is a pretty solid sign that something is seriously wrong.

If the circuit is up but the protocol is down, the router cannot understand the signals coming over the T1. If this is a brand-new circuit, it is probably misconfigured, but in mature circuits this may mean line noise or damage. (It can also mean that someone else somewhere along the circuit touched things, but no ISP or telco would even *dream* of doing that, not even if some underpaid and overworked tech thought you wouldn't notice if he just tweaked one setting while nobody was looking.)

Although you'll want to check the rest of the information available on this interface, there are things you can try first.

Resetting the Interface

First, if some network device along the circuit is confused, resetting the interface may kick that device back to its senses.

```
router#conf t
router(config)#int s1/0
router(config-int)#shut
```

Count to ten slowly, and then reopen the interface.

```
router(config-int)#no shut
router(config-int)#^Z
router#
```

If your circuit is back up, congratulations! If not, the next step is to reboot the router.

Rebooting the Router

While pulling the power cord out of the back, counting to ten, and plugging it back in will do the trick, as long as you're logged in you might as well restart the router in a slightly more graceful manner.

```
router# reload
```

The router will prompt you for confirmation and then restart itself. If your router has a separate CSU/DSU, power cycle it simultaneously.

Nothing Worked!

If neither of these works, you will have to phone your ISP or telco. You can make this call in one of two ways: either armed with lots of information so you can resolve the problem as quickly as possible, or in a hysterical panic. If you prefer the hysterical panic technique, make that call now. If not, arm yourself with all the information your router has to offer before calling. No matter how good your ISP's customer service department is, failure of your network is more important to *you* than it is to the person answering the phone. After all, that support tech still has *his* email!

When you make that call, however, you will sound much more impressive and serious if you can say, "Our circuit protocol has failed, and we are receiving hundreds of CRC errors a second," than if you say, "Uh, our circuit isn't working." Your router provides you with a wide range of debugging information, if you know how to read it.

Interface Debugging Information

Each router interface provides a full description of the work it is performing, the errors it sees, and what actions it is taking. While we won't cover every scrap of information your router offers, you should understand some of the basics when you have to troubleshoot. Here's the output from a sho int on a standard Cisco T1 interface. Your output might look slightly different, depending on your interface and circuit type.

NOTE *Input and Output*
Remember, a router's "input" is traffic that is entering the router via the interface, while the "output" is leaving the router via that interface. In the case of a T1, input is coming in from the outside world, while output is leaving your network and heading out over the T1. On a typical Ethernet interface, router input is leaving the local network, and output is arriving at the local network.

```
#sho int s1/0
...
❶   Last input 00:00:07, output 00:00:07, output hang never
❷   Last clearing of "show interface" counters 5w6d
...
❸   5 minute input rate 6000 bits/sec, 6 packets/sec
    5 minute output rate 6000 bits/sec, 2 packets/sec
❹   6413455 packets input, 2153942875 bytes, 0 no buffer
❺   Received 0 broadcasts, 0 runts, 641 giants, 0 throttles
❻   36851 input errors, 327 CRC, 36520 frame, 0 overrun, 0 ignored, 4 abort
    2871476 packets output, 608779651 bytes, 0 underruns
❼   0 output errors, 0 collisions, 31 interface resets
    0 output buffer failures, 0 output buffers swapped out
❽   27 carrier transitions
❾   DCD=up  DSR=up  DTR=up  RTS=up  CTS=up
```

The ❶ "last input" and "last output" values show how long it has been since packets entered or left this interface. This particular interface has been idle for seven seconds, which is not surprising with a problematic T1 or a slow network.

Cisco tracks most errors with an incrementing counter. The ❷ last clearing of "show interface" counters space shows the last time this incremental counter was reset to zero. In this example, the counters have been incrementing for five weeks and six days, far too long to be useful for troubleshooting a problem happening right now—those 15 million errors the router has recorded could have happened a month ago or in the last minute, and there's no way to tell. It's very easy to reset these counters, though, and you don't even have to go into configure mode:

```
router#clear counters
Clear "show interface" counters on all interfaces [confirm]
router#
```

All the counters will be reset to zero, for all interfaces. You can now do a sho int on your failed interface several times in succession and easily see if any error counters are increasing while the problem is happening. (Yes, you can do this while the error counters are all high, but it's much easier to see the difference between 0 and 300 than to see the difference between 15831594 and 15831894, especially if many error counters have nonzero values.)

Input/Output Rates

The ❸ five-minute input and output rates can be useful for troubleshooting. Although they are averaged over the last five minutes, you can check the interface several times in succession to see how they change. Is the average tending toward zero or climbing rapidly?

Remember, a T1 only handles 1.54MB/sec, or 1,540,000 bits per second. If your average throughput is close to that, that's why your network feels slow. A distributed denial-of-service attack or a sudden rush on your website can make your users feel like the Internet is down, when actually it's just a massive flood of traffic making your circuit useless. The ❹ totals of all packets processed since the counters were cleared can be useful in a similar way.

Types of Errors

The interface then gets ❺ specific on the types of errors it sees. *Broadcasts* are standard network broadcasts and generally are not a cause for alarm. *Runt* packets are smaller than the router's minimum packet size, and *giants* are larger than the maximum packet size. Neither should be on a T1 circuit. If they appear on an Ethernet segment, some network device is sending them out.

❻ *Input errors* cause packets to be rejected. The interface presents a total of all the input errors and then breaks them down by category. Although a certain number of errors is normal, if input errors comprise over one percent of your incoming packets, you have a problem. In this example, we have

36,000 input errors. We've input about 6.4 million packets, though, so this is far less than one percent of all packets, an acceptable error rate.

CRC and *frame input errors* probably indicate some sort of line noise; if these are happening frequently, call your ISP or telco and have them troubleshoot the circuit.

Overrun, ignored, and *abort input errors* indicate that the router cannot process incoming packets quickly enough and is forced to drop surplus packets. You can adjust the router's internal buffers, but this is very tricky to do correctly. I strongly encourage you to use Cisco's SmartNet support and have a technician help you adjust the buffers to fit your particular situation.

❼ *Output errors* are most common on an Ethernet interface, where an extremely high collision rate can interfere with the network's performance. On a serial line, output errors are most commonly the result of running out of buffers for outgoing packets (though this is quite rare on small routers). Again, if you're consistently running out of buffers, contact Cisco for help.

Using Carrier Transition to Detect a Bad Serial Connection

One of the more useful ways to detect a bad serial connection is the ❽ *carrier transitions* line. A carrier transition is when the interface either goes up or comes down. It's entirely possible for a serial line to bounce up and down so quickly that you won't catch it by successive sho int commands. The carrier transition increments whenever the line goes down, and again whenever it comes back up. By watching this field, you can detect an unstable circuit.

Finally, a serial line will list the ❾ signals that it is receiving over the line. For the line to be functional, all of these need to be up; if any are not up even after rebooting everything, call your ISP or telco. Your router cannot process traffic it cannot hear!

Extended Pings and Circuit Troubleshooting

Cisco routers can use a variety of ping tests to check IP connectivity to other networks. This is very useful for testing troublesome serial circuits that are not down but that are not actually working properly. At times, a misprovisioned circuit will cause problems that do not appear on sho int, but that cause no end of headaches.

On more than one occasion, I've dealt with a circuit with a perfect-looking interface that passed every standard ping test with flying colors and yet was useless. GIF files could not be moved across these circuits and Windows networking infrastructure protocols would not work over them. In each case, the problem was exactly the same: the circuit was provisioned incorrectly (with AMI encoding instead of the modern standard of B8ZS). This meant that the circuit could not pass large all-zero packets. The .gif image format uses a lot of large all-zero packets, as do the Windows network protocols.

NOTE *Other physical errors generate different symptoms; this particular example is just the one that seems destined to haunt me. Your data circuit should accept whatever sort of data you want to transmit, even if it is a whole lot of nothing!*

To perform an extended ping test, enter enable mode and just type **ping**.

```
router#ping
Protocol [ip]:
Target IP address: 192.168.5.3
```

The default protocol is IP, so just press ENTER. Then give the IP address you want to ping. Generally, this is the IP address of the router on the other side of your serial link.

Don't use pings to Internet sites to test your circuit's status; that tests every link between your router and the remote Internet site! The other end of the circuit is the only reasonable place to ping when testing your own circuit's behavior.

```
Repeat count [5]: 1000
```

When using extended ping, use more than five pings. A few hundred is the bare minimum for this sort of test, but a thousand is usually reasonable. Either your test will be over in just a few seconds, or you'll be interrupting it anyway. If you sweep the range of sizes (as recommended later), the router will decide how many pings are necessary to properly cover the range, and the value you enter here will be ignored anyway.

```
Datagram size [100]:
```

You could specify a size here if you wished, but we'll be doing something slightly more advanced in the extended commands.

```
Timeout in seconds [2]:
```

Two seconds is a very reasonable timeout. Giving a longer timeout is generally useless for most IP circuits, because either the packet will return in much less time, or you'll wait that much longer for failed packets. With a shorter timeout, you may miss perfectly legitimate return packets that are delayed by a busy remote router.

```
Extended commands [n]: y
```

If you take the default n (no) here, the router will run the ping as you have specified it. But most of the truly nifty options are in the extended commands, so enter y for yes.

```
Source address or interface:
```

With loose source rerouting, you can change your source IP address and send packets from a particular interface, which is useful to do on backbone routers but not for most small offices. I highly recommend that you don't try this, because the results will only confuse you. (Tracking down problems is difficult enough without using an easily misunderstood tool!)

```
Type of service [0]:
Set DF bit in IP header? [no]:
Validate reply data? [no]:
```

These three flags manipulate or verify TCP/IP data but aren't generally useful for day-to-day work. If you're not familiar with the innards of TCP/IP, just take the defaults.

```
Data pattern [0xABCD]: 0xffff
```

A ping packet contains four bytes, and you can choose what data to put in them. The hexadecimal 0xABCD is the default, but two common choices are 0x0000 (all zeros) and 0xFFFF (all ones). Many misconfigured circuits fail with certain sizes of all-zero or all-one packets.

```
Loose, Strict, Record, Timestamp, Verbose[none]:
```

You can choose to use loose or strict source rerouting, record the route taken by the ping packets, datestamp each ping packet, or use verbose output. If you don't know what loose or strict source routing are, don't try to use them. For most situations, almost none of these are useful, but you might try verbose output sometime for your own edification; just enter **v** at the prompt.

```
Sweep range of sizes [n]: y
```

By sweeping the range of sizes, you send packets ranging from very small to quite large. Definitely set this when testing a troublesome circuit. The smaller packets will appear quickly, larger packets much more slowly. If you sweep the range of sizes, the ping command will ignore the count you entered earlier; you will need to interrupt it with CTRL-^.

```
Sweep min size [36]:
Sweep max size [18024]:
```

These are the minimum and maximum packet sizes when sweeping. The defaults range from quite tiny to reasonably large.

```
Sweep interval [1]: 50
```

The sweep interval is the increment to the packet size when sweeping. For example, with the example shown here, the first packet sent will be 36 bytes, the second 37 bytes, the third 38, and so on, until a packet size of 18,024 is reached. Picking a larger increment than 1 will accelerate the test. Also, you may not want to let your router send 17,092 pings to perform the test with every possible sized packet in the range.

Once you have chosen all the values, the ping will run.

```
Type escape sequence to abort.
Sending 1800, [36..18024]-byte ICMP Echos to 198.88.118.11, timeout is 2
seconds:
Packet has data pattern 0xFFFF
!!!!!!!!!!!!!!!!!!!!!!!!!!!!!!!!!!!!!!!!!!!!!!!!!!!!!!!!!!!!!!!!!!!!!!!!!!!!
...
```

Each exclamation point indicates a successful ping, while a period indicates a missed one. This ping test will continue until the 1800 packets have been sent. Reducing the increment will increase the number of pings the router sends. Again, you can interrupt the test at any time by pressing CTRL-^.

For circuits that are behaving poorly or exhibiting "weird" behavior, I suggest running the extended ping test three times: once with the default data pattern, once with an all-zero data pattern, and once with all ones. If your circuit has trouble with certain sorts of packets, this process will probably uncover it. If not, your circuit is probably running cleanly.

Phoning the ISP

So you've opted to gather all your debugging information before calling. You know which sorts of errors are appearing on your circuit, and what sort of packets your circuit will and will not pass. Now what?

You got your T1 circuit from either a telco or an ISP. Phone them. The first words out of your mouth should be, "I have a down circuit." When you reach a technical support person, explain:

- The state of the line itself (both line and protocol down, or just protocol down, or both line and protocol up)

- That you have rebooted your router and CSU/DSU (this will almost certainly be their first suggestion)

- The types of errors you are seeing: CRC, framing, overruns, aborts, and so on

- The results of any ping tests you have run

The technician should check the ISP's end of the circuit and phone the telco who originally provisioned the line. Most telephone companies will return a call to the circuit owner (usually the ISP) within an hour with an initial status report.

NOTE *While your ISP should handle circuit issues, especially when they own the circuit, if the problem is actually a failed circuit, it may take hours to repair.*

Circuit Loopback Tests

T1 circuits include all sorts of intelligent equipment such as repeaters, switches, and smartjacks. The telco can talk to this equipment using a series of successive loopback tests to quickly identify where a problem lies and what piece of equipment is at fault.

The telco has a diagram listing every piece of equipment along a circuit. A loopback test is where they attempt to communicate with each piece of equipment in succession. For example, the telco central office will try to "loop up" the first piece of equipment outside their office—say, the repeater in the little gray box up the street. If they can easily communicate with that device, and if that device can return data it receives to the central office, they will loop up the second closest device and test it. When something fails to respond, they send a technician out to examine and repair that device.

Eventually, the telco will work their way down to looping up the smartjack at your demarc. If the telco can communicate correctly with the smartjack, they will probably try to loop up your CSU/DSU. The telco/ISP's responsibility technically ends at the smartjack, but they will frequently try to go the extra step simply to demonstrate that it isn't their problem. (This tactic should be painfully familiar to anyone who has worked a help desk!) If the telco says that they can cleanly loop up the smart-jack, but cannot loop up the CSU/DSU, the problem lies somewhere between the CSU/DSU and the smartjack and is unquestionably your problem.

This sort of exhaustive test takes time, especially on a long circuit, but it is the quickest way to identify a problem. The telco may have to send a technician out to your facility to perform testing. You may well have to have someone stay after hours to let the technician in and out of the building.

WARNING *A loopback test will completely disable your circuit! If your circuit is already down, then they can loopback all they want, but if you are merely suffering degraded performance, you may want to ask the ISP or telco to perform the test after hours. It's all a question of what your environment requires.*

Once you know without a doubt that the problem is with the telco or the ISP, the only skill required to fix the issue is a willingness to make a nuisance of yourself at the ISP's help desk.

If It's Your Problem

If the ISP can loop up the smartjack but not your router, it's your problem. Congratulations! The good news is, as you have very few components in your section of the circuit, testing your equipment won't take very long. The bad news is, many components you do have will require outside help.

Check to make sure everything in your system is tightly attached. A loose connection can cause no end of problems. "Is it plugged in?" is still a good question in the comms closet.

A common culprit in circuit failures is wiring. Replace the wiring between the smartjack and your CSU/DSU. A T1 circuit uses a standard Cat 5 cable, so many people plug in a cable that they had in a drawer somewhere. A T1 is less forgiving than Ethernet, however. Try using a good premade cable, with solid connectors on both ends.

If you've replaced all your wiring, and everything is firmly seated, and reboots and resets have not solved your problem, phone your CSU/DSU's technical support line. On a modern Cisco system, this would be Cisco itself.

NOTE *If your vendors start each blaming the other, as is common among lower-level technical support staff, do not be afraid to get them all on the phone at once and let them fight it out.*

Now that you know how to troubleshoot your router, you can learn how to upgrade it.

6

IOS CHANGES

Cisco's Internetwork Operating System (IOS) is the brains of any Cisco router; it provides the command line, interface device drivers, routing software, and all the other bits that make a router do more than draw power and generate heat. Cisco continuously maintains and updates IOS, adding more features as they become useful and stable. If you want some of Cisco's nifty new functionality, you'll probably find it in an IOS upgrade.

The only reasons to upgrade are for security, stability, or required features. While it might be cool to have the latest IOS, that is insufficient motivation for staying up all night hoping that a "bad upgrade recovery process" works. I advise you to find any technical justification you can to not perform an upgrade. A successful upgrade only causes a few minutes of downtime, but a failed upgrade can take the router out of action for several hours.

NOTE *SmartNet and IOS Upgrades*
Do not attempt an IOS upgrade without a SmartNet support agreement! An IOS upgrade gone bad may leave your router completely unusable without advanced help. I've had upgrades where the router could not find its own network interfaces, or wouldn't boot at all and was stuck in rommon (BIOS) mode. Cisco has many different versions of IOS for each router, and installing the wrong IOS can turn your expensive router into an expensive chunk of metal and plastic that requires expert help to repair.

If everything goes perfectly, the upgrade process is quick and easy: get the new IOS file onto the router's flash disk and reboot.

Cisco Security Notifications

Every so often, some bright person discovers a security flaw in the Cisco IOS. Because the router is the first point of entry onto a network, no security device on your network can protect it, which means that when a security hole is discovered in IOS, you may have to upgrade the router to keep intruders out.

Cisco announces security issues through a customer mailing list and through security mailing lists such as BugTraq.

If you're not already on a mailing list that gets Cisco security announcements, you should sign up for Cisco's customer security announcements list, cust-security-announce@cisco.com. Send an email containing *only* the words "subscribe cust-security-announce" to majordomo@cisco.com. You'll receive a reply giving you instructions on how to confirm your subscription.

Read all Cisco security alerts carefully. If you're not using the targeted functionality mentioned in an alert, or if the problem doesn't affect your equipment, don't worry about it. But if the alert affects you, schedule a maintenance window to take the router down and upgrade the IOS.

Upgrade Preparations

Before upgrading, make sure that you have an FTP server available close to the router. (The official Cisco documentation discusses using a TFTP server, but an FTP server is far more secure and no more difficult to use than a TFTP server.) You'll need a user account and password on that FTP server along with a few megs of disk space. (If you don't have FTP server software, you'll find dozens of free ones on sites like http://www.tucows.com and http://www.freshmeat.net.)

An emergency Internet connection is also useful in case something goes wrong. Although Cisco has extensive disaster recovery documentation on its website, it will be largely useless if you don't have Internet access! By setting up an account with a dial-up ISP for one of your workstations, you'll be able to access this information easily. A number of ISPs allow their users a certain number of dial-up hours free each month; I have a NetZero account set up at the office for exactly this purpose.

Finally, confirm that you have a Cisco console cable and that it works. If the upgrade goes really, really badly, you may have to console in to restore service.

IOS Versions

Once you have these trivialities out of the way, you'll need a new IOS image to install. Cisco's IOS is released in several parallel versions, each with a unique version number. For example, "12.0" is an older release, "12.1" is a later version, "13.0" is more recent still, and so on. You know the drill.

- Each release is available in a variety of patch levels, indicated in parenthesis after the main release number, like 12.0(7). (This may not be the seventh release of version 12.0, by the way; you'll also see further divisions, such as 12.0(5)a and 12.0(5)b.)

- Cisco adds capital letters to the end of the release name to indicate special branches or versions of a particular IOS release, as in 12.0(7)XK. These letters may change as features are shuffled from branch to branch. (It is possible—but not easy—to track a particular set of features from version to version and release to release.)

Choosing Your IOS Version

Because of the various ways that IOS images are labeled, choosing the new IOS image to install on your router is often the trickiest part of the upgrade. You'll want an IOS version that contains all the necessary device drivers for your hardware, with support for the features you require.

The simplest way to get the correct IOS version is to open a Technical Assistance Request at Cisco's website. Run show tech on your router, capture the output, and attach it to your request so that your support tech will have everything he needs to make an informed decision. Cisco usually responds to these requests within hours with a custom link to the exact image you need.

Cisco also provides the Software Advisor Web tool, which purports to guide you to the correct version of IOS for your exact hardware. More than once, I've used this tool and found that the version I downloaded won't work on my router; either the router refuses to boot with that IOS image, or the new IOS won't recognize some of my router interfaces. Feel free to try it, if you're into recovering damaged systems or if risking router failure under load gives you a warm, fuzzy feeling.

One way or another, you'll get a file containing the new IOS version. This file is called an *image*. Put your new IOS image on your FTP server. Do not change the file's name.

Find the Current IOS Image

If your shiny new IOS image doesn't work the way Cisco promises, you'll want to be able to fall back to your current IOS version and router configuration so you can at least restore service. The current version is somewhere on your router's flash disk. As shown in Chapter 2, the image name that the router booted with is shown in the show version output. Perhaps half a dozen lines down in the show version output you'll see the System image file entry.

```
...
System image file is "❶flash:❷c3640-is56i-mz-120-7-XK1"
...
```

The image file is stored on ❶ internal flash and is ❷ named c3640-is56i-mz-120-7-XK1. This is the file you want to back up.

Viewing Disk Contents

Go into enable mode and enter `dir /all`.

```
router# dir /all
Directory of flash:/

 1  -rw-     9270984            <no date>  ❶c3640-is56i-mz-120-7-XK1.bin
 2  -rw-          25            <no date>  snmpengineid

❷33554432 bytes total (❸24283292 bytes free)
```

There's only one file on this router, our ❶ boot image. There isn't enough room on this flash device to store another image—we have ❷ used more space with the existing image than we have left ❸ free. While this particular router has two slots for flash cards, neither slot has a card in it.

If you have a router with PCMCIA slots for flash memory, I highly recommend that you purchase a Cisco-branded flash card. Although they cost a few hundred dollars, it will make recovering from a failed upgrade much, much easier. (Regular flash cards will almost certainly not work with a Cisco router; don't even bother trying them.)

Copying Files

The `copy` command duplicates an existing file elsewhere, just like its DOS equivalent. The syntax is

```
router# copy <current location> <new location>
```

The difficult part is knowing the syntax for the various locations you might be copying from. Copying from one filesystem to another is perhaps the easiest; all you need is the full path to each filename. For example, if we have an IOS image on flash that we want to copy to a flash card in slot 0, we would just use

```
router#copy flash:c3640-is56i-mz-120-7-XK1.bin slot0:c3640-is56i-mz-120-7-XK1.bin
```

By doing this, you've backed up your current IOS to a removable flash card for safekeeping. In the event that your shiny new IOS image doesn't boot, you can pull the known working image off the flash disk and rapidly restore service.

If you're not lucky enough to have a flash card, you can copy the current image to your FTP server. The Cisco FTP client will not prompt you for a username and password for your FTP server, however, so you need to give it on the command line as part of the copy command. An FTP location for the copy command looks like this:

```
ftp://username:password@servername/filename
```

So, assume you have an FTP server running on the machine fileserver. Your account name is mwlucas, and the password is YrtIwuarph?[1] To copy an image from the flash drive to the FTP server, you would issue the following command.

```
router# copy flash:c3640-is56i-mz-120-7-XK1.bin
ftp://mwlucas:YrtIwuarph?@fileserver/c3640-is56i-mz-120-7-XK1.bin
Address or name of remote host [fileserver]?
Destination filename [c3640-is56i-mz-120-7-XK1.bin]?
Writing c3640-is56i-mz-120-7-XK1.bin
!!!!!!!!!!!!!!!!!!!!!!!!!!!!!!!!!!!!!!!!!!!!!!!!!!!!!!
....
router#
```

The router prompts you to confirm the server name and the destination filename. Just press ENTER if you gave the correct locations on the command line, or you can correct them here. (You cannot enter or correct the username or password interactively, however; that would be too convenient.)

It's also a good idea to back up your router's configuration in case the upgrade goes really, really badly and the router loses its memory. You can simply use a text file backup if you wish, or you can actually FTP the startup configuration to the FTP server.

```
router# copy startup-config ftp://mwlucas:YrtIwuarph?@fileserver/startup-config
```

When you have backed up your current system, you are finished until your maintenance window begins.

---

[1] This is, of course, an acronym for "You really think I would use a real password here?"

Performing the Upgrade

An IOS upgrade requires a router reboot, which interrupts service. If all goes well, the router will only be down for a few minutes. If the new IOS image does not work, you will need to reload the old IOS onto the router and reboot again. If you have an external flash card, or if you have enough room on the router's flash memory to store multiple IOS images, you'll be able to restore the old image fairly quickly. If you don't have those features, you will need to get the old IOS image onto the router either via FTP, or if your router no longer knows it has network interfaces, via xmodem over a serial cable. Allow yourself at least two hours for this recovery process.

In short, schedule a two-hour (or longer!) window of acceptable downtime for a router upgrade.

IOS Installation

After all of this work, the new IOS installation itself is almost anticlimactic. Just copy the image from the FTP server to the router's internal flash.

```
router# copy ftp://username:password@servername/new-image-name
flash:new-image-name
```

The copy command will prompt you for confirmation. If the internal flash is too small to hold both the old image and the new image, it will ask you if you want to erase the existing flash first. Confirm that you really do have a backup of the old IOS image, and then proceed to erase the flash.

After the image file is loaded onto the router's flash storage, reload the router. The router should boot with the new IOS. You can confirm this with show version upon the next reboot.

Managing Multiple IOS Images

If you are one of the lucky people with a router that has enough flash to hold multiple IOS images, you don't want to erase the entire flash just to make room for the new image. The erase command will erase a particular file from a storage device, making room for the new image. Usually, you'll have two image files on the flash: the version you're currently running and the previous version. To fit a new image on the flash, erase the oldest image you have.

```
router# erase flash:filename
```

You should now have enough room to load the new IOS image.

When the router has enough internal flash to hold multiple IOS images, it will automatically boot with the first available image. Do a `dir flash:` to determine what image that is. If the wrong image is first, you can hard-code the image to be booted with a `boot system` command.

```
router#conf t
router(config)#no boot system
router(config)#boot system flash imagename
router(config)^z
```

Disaster Recovery

If your new IOS image is bad, upon a reboot the router may be unstable; it might not know it has any network interfaces, it might repeatedly crash, or it might even only boot into "rommon" mode—the Cisco equivalent of "Press F2 for Setup."

If you are in this situation but have your old version of IOS available on the router itself (either on flash or on a flash card), boot the old image. This will at least restore service while you get Cisco on the phone and make use of your SmartNet contract to have them help you fix the problem.

If you do not have the old IOS handy on the router itself—say, it's backed up on your FTP server instead—you must load the image back onto the router via xmodem over your console cable. The process for this varies with router types and failure types, so we won't go into detail here. I suggest that you immediately phone Cisco and open a Priority 1 case. The magic words are, "I am completely down." When the Cisco tech understands that your router is off the Internet and you are totally hosed, they will be able to immediately connect you to a technician who can point you to the correct recovery procedure for your router. They will even hold your hand and walk you through every step of the process if you desire. Even though I've had upgrades fail several times, and I know what to do for each of my routers, when time is running short it's nice to have an expert on the phone.

Now that you can upgrade your router, let's look at providing backup connectivity.

7

REDUNDANCY WITH
BGP AND HSRP

The component of your Internet service most likely to fail is your Internet circuit. Cisco routers can use multiple Internet circuits from multiple providers, giving your network the best possible access to Internet sites and other Internet users the best possible access to your company.

This is possible through the Border Gateway Protocol (BGP). BGP announces to the whole world what IP addresses your router is responsible for, and it listens to other routers to learn the best way to reach other sites. BGP is not difficult to understand or to implement, but it has its own tricks and traps. You may want to do additional research into how to make BGP meet your particular needs, but this section will be enough to get you up and running with multiple Internet providers.

BGP Basics

The key to BGP is the *Autonomous System (AS)*. An AS is a single network, of any size, that makes its own routing decisions. If your company has only one route onto the Internet, your network makes no routing decisions—it dumps everything across that single route. If your network had two routes onto the Internet, via two different providers, your network would have to decide where to send each chunk of traffic, and you could adjust how traffic entered and left your network. You would be an autonomous system. Similarly, huge companies such as Level3 and MCI are autonomous systems. Every AS is assigned an Autonomous System Number, or ASN, to uniquely identify that autonomous system on the Internet. Autonomous systems exchange routing information via BGP. Two autonomous systems that connect directly to each other and exchange routing information are said to *peer*.

Take a look at our sample network of autonomous systems (Figure 7-1). This sample is much smaller and much less interconnected than the real Internet, but it's good enough to use to understand the basic principles. Your network is AS100 and peers with AS200 and AS300. AS300 in turn peers with AS200, AS400, AS500, and AS600.

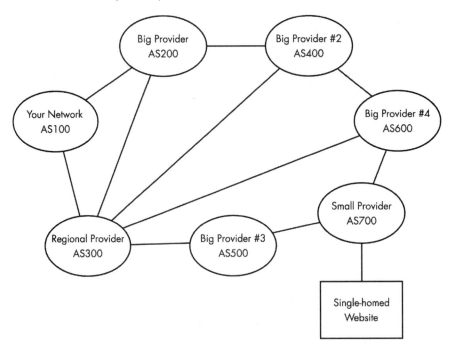

Figure 7-1: A sample network of Autonomous Systems

Each AS tells its peers what IP addresses can be reached in that AS. For example, if your company has the block of IP addresses 192.168.8.0 through 192.168.8.255, your router would tell AS200 and AS300 that they should send packets bound for those IP addresses to your network. This is called a *route announcement*. Every route announcement you receive from a peer uses a small chunk of memory.

Similarly, each of your peers tells your router what routes can be reached through their networks, and what networks your packets will pass through to reach their destinations. For example, your AS200 peer would tell you that to reach the website behind AS700, your packets will travel through AS200, AS400, AS600, and AS700. This chain of AS numbers is called an *AS path*.

Your router will make its decisions on where to send packets based on the AS path. To reach the target website via the AS200 peer, your packets will have to travel through four autonomous systems. To reach the target website via the AS300 peer, the packets will travel through only three autonomous systems. Because the AS path is shorter via the AS300 peer, BGP dictates that your router will send packets bound for that website via AS300.

When you configure BGP, you must decide how much routing information you want to receive from each peer. *Full routes* means that your peer will send you everything it knows about every network on the Internet. *Partial routes* means that the peer will only send you routes for networks directly attached to that network. *No routes* means that your router receives no routing information from that peer. The main reason to choose less than full routes from a peer is to reduce memory usage; in this case, you normally choose full routes from the smaller peer and partial routes from the larger peer, or if you're *really* tight on memory you might take partial routes from the smaller peer and no routes from the larger, and choose to use the larger peer as your default route, assuming that the larger peer will have more directly connected networks than your smaller peer.

Routes are designed to cover as many IP addresses as possible in a single route statement. Major ISPs announce blocks /16 or larger whenever possible. The smallest route announcement that will be accepted by the global Internet is a /24 (what used to be called a "class C" network). To use BGP, your network must have at least a /24 address block.[1]

---

[1] If any of this paragraph confuses you, read the appendix.

What BGP Isn't

BGP is not a load-balancing protocol. If you have two Internet circuits, BGP will not divide the load evenly between them. However, BGP will achieve a similar effect by choosing the best AS path to send packets out on. But if one provider is far better connected than the other, the better provider will be chosen every single time, resulting in asymmetric circuit usage.

BGP neither knows nor cares about capacity, speed, or congestion when making routing decisions. In our earlier example, to reach the single-homed website in Figure 7-1, we would choose to go via AS300 because it's only three AS hops away. BGP doesn't know that part of AS300 is on a satellite link to a router in Burma, where the packets are collected daily and delivered via camel courier to their colocation with the next AS in the chain. All BGP cares about is the AS path.

BGP doesn't tell remote people what choice to make when trying to reach your network. In Figure 7-1, AS400 is two hops away by either AS200 or AS300. You might have a DS3 to AS300 and a T1 to AS200, and would therefore prefer that people enter your network via AS300. If so, too bad; it's not BGP's place to tell people these things. (You can use a BGP trick to work around that, mind you, but it's certainly neither reliable nor fine-grained.)

Keep these facts in mind when troubleshooting routing issues. For example, it's natural to think that BGP does load balancing—you have two circuits, and BGP spreads the load between them, after all! But that thinking will trap you when you need to figure out why packets are going in a certain way.

BGP Preparations

To run BGP, you must have the following:

- A router with more than 128MB of RAM.
- Two ISPs, both willing to provide you with a BGP feed.
- An IOS version that supports BGP version 4.
- A block of IP addresses /24 or larger. Several smaller chunks that add up to a /24 are useless for BGP.
- An Autonomous System Number.
- A routing registry entry for your network block.

We'll look at each in turn.

Router Features

Let's dispose of the easy requirement first. Your router must have an IOS image that supports BGP. If your IOS doesn't support BGP, use your SmartNet contract to get a version that does.

Memory is a little more problematical. Each route announcement from a peer takes up a little bit of memory. When you are receiving full routes from two peers, your routing table will use most of your router's free memory. Attempting to use any advanced Cisco router features will overflow your router's memory and cause problems. The global routing table grows every year. In 2004, a recent IOS image and two full routing tables almost completely filled 128MB of RAM, and soon more than 128MB will be required to run BGP with full routes from two peers.

You can reduce memory usage by taking only partial routes from one peer. Your router will only send packets meant for that peer to that peer, and will send everything else to the other peer. This only aggravates the problem of asymmetrical bandwidth use, however, unless you are directly connected to a network with a major client or have some other heavy bandwidth requirement directly connected to that peer.

Oddly enough, Cisco routers that can only handle 128MB of RAM are becoming *much* easier to find on eBay. People are selling them for a reason. I highly recommend that you start with 256MB of RAM if at all possible.

ISPs with BGP

Believe it or not, many small ISPs have only a single circuit to the Internet. These ISPs do not have BGP feeds and cannot provide you with one either. When shopping for an ISP for multihoming, be certain to ask if they can provide a BGP feed. Also ask your current provider if they provide that service. It's possible that multihoming will require you to terminate your current Internet service contract and sign new ones with two entirely different providers.

Ask your providers for their AS numbers; you must have them to get your own ASN.

IP Addresses

Remember, national backbones filter all route announcements smaller than /24. You must have a block of addresses at least that large to use BGP. Several smaller chunks that add up to the same size are *not* sufficient. If you do not currently have that large a block of addresses, talk with the salesperson for your second connection. Chances are that the ISP will be willing to issue you a sufficiently large block of IP addresses to run BGP in order to get your business—after all, without the addresses you don't need a second circuit! They might charge you for your IP addresses, however.

You must have at least one block /24 or larger to get an ASN.

Getting an ASN

The American Registry for Internet Numbers (ARIN) assigns Autonomous System Numbers in the Western Hemisphere. (If you are elsewhere in the world, you will have your own regional number administration.) The application process is very simple, *if* you have everything ready before applying. ARIN's website at http://www.arin.net has documentation on the ASN request process and a blank template.

Only organizations registered with ARIN can request an ASN. Registering an organization is free and gives your organization an ARIN organization ID, or *Org ID*. You use the Org ID as a point of contact for the ASN request form. You can get the request form from the ARIN website. As an organization brand new to ARIN, you *must* use the detailed Org ID request form. The request form is plain text; everything after a pound sign (#) is a comment, while every place there is a colon is a place you are expected to put an answer. Example answers appear below the question where appropriate. We're not going to walk through the entire Org ID request form, because the questions it asks are very basic: names, addresses, phone numbers, and so on. Send the completed form to hostmaster@arin.net with a subject of "ORGANIZATION TEMPLATE."

Within a few days, you should receive a notice that your organization has been registered and giving the details of your organization's information. One important piece of information is your new org handle, which contains an alphanumeric code for your organization. Each contact you defined for your organization will also receive a handle. Note the handle codes, because you'll need them to request your ASN. (If you forget your handles, you can use the Whois search engine on the ARIN website to search for your organization's entry.)

When you have an Org ID, you can fill out an ASN request template. Because some of the questions can be tricky, we'll walk through the current version of the form.

These first two questions are obviously designed to weed out the people who don't need an ASN. If you're not multihomed, or if you are multihomed but don't need BGP, you don't need an ASN.

List the address range(s) you will be announcing via BGP. These must be real, public addresses issued to you from one of your ISPs. If your addresses are not announceable via BGP (i.e., if you list IP addresses designated for internal use only), the request will be denied.

Question 4 wants the ASNs of your ISPs, which your ISPs can easily provide. You must give two valid ASNs.

It is theoretically possible to get an ASN without multihoming, but if you're in that situation, you didn't buy this book to learn how to do it. Leave this blank.

I strongly recommend that you leave this blank. Answering questions 1 through 4 properly is all you need to justify receiving an ASN.

Enter the org handle your organization received from ARIN.

This should exactly match the organization name you registered previously.

Create an alphanumeric handle for your ASN. This will appear in the ARIN database, and will be used to uniquely identify your

AS. Use the Whois search at http://www.arin.net to ensure nobody already has that handle.

You can specify additional contacts by ARIN handle in the remaining fields, but this is not necessary. Mail your form to hostmaster@arin.net, with a subject of "ASN REQUEST." Within three business days, ARIN will either approve or reject your request. If they approve it, you have 60 days to complete the Terms of Service agreement and pay the fee (currently $500). If you are rejected, it's probably because you didn't fill out your request correctly. Read the rejection messages carefully and try again.

Routing Registries

Many large backbones use routing registries to identify which blocks of IP addresses should be announced by which ASNs. This prevents someone from destroying a company's Internet connectivity by sending out bogus route announcements for their IP addresses. The original Routing Arbiter Database (RADB) is maintained by Merit, but today many backbones have their own RADB systems.

Check with your ISPs. They may or may not require that you register with a RADB, and they may or may not have particular RADBs that they will accept. Because each RADB differs, there's no point in going through a detailed exercise in filling out forms. The best advice that I can give is to read the instructions carefully and look at samples of other entries in that registry for examples.

After you reach the point where your IP addresses are registered in a RADB, you can actually configure BGP on your router.

Configuring BGP

The good news is that the paperwork necessary to prepare for BGP is the hard part. The actual setup process is very mechanical. When you configure BGP, your ISP should provide you with an IP address for their router's BGP session (usually, their end of the Internet circuit) and an ASN to peer with.

Your Address Announcements

By default, a BGP session refuses to announce routes to its peers. This helps prevent a small company's router from becoming an inter-backbone exchange point. (Your upstream providers should filter your announcements so that they only receive the proper routes from you, so this shouldn't be a problem.[2]) For a router to announce a block of addresses via BGP, it must know where to send packets bound for those addresses when a peer sends them. In a small network, the simplest way to do this is to provide a single static route for the exact block of addresses you want to announce to your peers. Providing several static routes for pieces of that block is insufficient: you *must* have a single route for the entire block.

The easiest thing to do is provide a static route for the whole announced block to the "null0" interface. While null0 is only a logical interface that exists only to discard data, your router will use a more specific route if one is available. This monolithic route also allows you to renumber router interfaces or change how your subnets are routed without worrying about scrambling BGP's route announcements.

Configuring Addresses for Announcement

For example, assume that you have the address block 192.168.0.0/23 on your network. The first half of that block is attached to your router's Ethernet interface, while the second half is routed to a firewall further into your network. Obviously, your router knows where to send packets bound for any individual IP address within that block. It doesn't know where to send the block as a whole, however. While both halves of the network address block are routed, you must have a single static route for the whole of 192.168.0.0/23.

```
router(config)# ❶ip route 192.168.0.0 255.255.254.0 Null0
router(config)# access-list ❷130 ❸permit ip host ❹192.168.0.0 host ❺255.255.254.0
```

The first entry is a ❶ standard route statement, just as we discussed in Chapter 4. The second statement defines an access list, a completely new topic. Thick books have been written entirely about Cisco access lists, and we're not going to go over them in any great detail. (They are worth knowing, but they do need a book at least this large to do them even a faint hint of justice.) The important thing now is the syntax used for BGP route announcements. Every access list has a ❷ unique number, and the number defines the syntax of the remainder of the access list statement. For BGP, use a number between 100 and 199. The ❸ permit keyword tells us that this access list allows a

---

[2] Note the words "should" and "shouldn't" in this sentence. Sadly, some companies still don't do this basic filtering. A good ISP will.

certain type of traffic. We then need the ❹ network number and the ❺ netmask for the IP range we want to announce.

Configuring BGP

Once you have your addresses in static routes and access lists, you can tell BGP to announce them.

```
router(config)# ❶router ❷bgp ❸100
router(❹config-route)#
```

In configure mode, tell the router you want to ❶ enable ❷ BGP for ❸ your ASN. Note the change of ❹ command prompt when you begin BGP configuration. Then you can perform the initial setup of your BGP configuration.

```
router(config-route)# bgp ❶dampening
router(config-route)# ❷redistribute static
router(config-route)# ❸network 192.168.0.0 mask 255.255.254.0
```

BGP ❶ dampening allows your router to better resist *route flap*, which is when a route is repeatedly added to the routing table and then quickly withdrawn several times a minute. If one of your peers starts flapping, your router may become overloaded and crash. It's enabled by default on most modern IOS versions, but you should be absolutely sure it's there.

We then tell BGP to announce routes that it learned from ❷ static routing. (It's entirely possible to redistribute routes learned via other routing protocols, but you need a thicker book to learn how to do that safely.) Because your router might have many static routes, we need to specify exactly which ❸ routes we want to announce. We don't want to try to announce every little subnet that the router knows about, after all!

When you actually have a peer configured, it should see these routes.

Your First Neighbor

Now that you have prepared the routes you want to announce, configure an actual BGP session with one neighbor. You must have the peer's ASN and the IP address of the peer. Still in a "BGP 100" configure session, tell the router about a peer with the neighbor keyword.

```
router(config-route)#  neighbor ❶10.1.8.5 ❷remote-as 200
router(config-route)#  neighbor 10.1.8.5 ❸route-map ❹ispA-out ❺out
```

Identify each peer by the ❶ IP address you're peering with. Every line that applies to a single peer starts with the `neighbor ip address` statement. In a simple BGP setup, each peer only needs two bits of information: the ❷ AS of the remote side, and a ❸ route map used to identify permitted traffic. Like access lists, route maps are very powerful tools that require a lot of education to use to their full potential, but we'll cover just enough to get BGP working. I recommend ❹ naming each route map after the ISP you are peering with, with the suffix -out appended. The final word in the route-map configuration, ❺ out, indicates that this route map is only applied to outbound traffic.

Repeat this process for your second peer, identifying it by its unique IP address. Give this peer a unique route map name, such as `ispB-out`. When you have configured all your peers, ^Z out of configuration mode.

Route Maps

Our BGP configuration references route maps, but they don't exist yet. Go into plain configure mode, not a "BGP 100" session.

```
router(config)# route-map ❶ispA-out ❷permit ❸10
router(config-route)# ❹match ❺ip address ❻130
```

First create the route map ❶ named in the BGP rule and declare it is a ❷ permit rule, which means that it describes traffic allowed to pass. Although each route map can have several ❸ numbered instances, BGP we only needs one instance of the route map—but the number is still required.

Then define the traffic that this rule affects. We want this rule to apply to traffic that ❹ matches a particular ❺ IP address—in this case, the IP addresses defined in ❻ access list 130. We set up access list 130 when configuring address announcements. Do not attempt to put actual IP addresses here; it just won't work.

The combination of BGP route mapping and access list means that IP addresses that match 192.168.0.0/23 are permitted to be passed over the BGP session—in other words, BGP is allowed to announce those routes. This certainly seems obtuse if you're not familiar with route mapping and access lists, but simply filling in the correct IP addresses and ASN numbers will give you a working BGP setup.

A Complete BGP Configuration

When you're finished, your BGP configuration should look like the sample below. If any piece of this configuration is missing, BGP will not work. The most common problem in configuring BGP is forgetting one step of the configuration process. Compare a troublesome router configuration to the sample here, and add anything that's missing.

```
router bgp 100❶
 bgp dampening
 network 192.168.0.0 mask 255.255.254.0❷
 redistribute static❸
 neighbor 10.1.8.5 remote-as 200❹
 neighbor 10.1.8.5 route-map ispA-out out
 neighbor 172.16.0.2 remote-as 300❺
 neighbor 172.16.0.2 route-map ispB-out out
ip route 192.168.0.0 255.255.254.0 Null0❻
access-list 130 permit ip host 192.168.0.0 host 255.255.254.0❼
route-map ispA-out❽
 match ip address 130
route-map ispB-out❾
 match ip address 130
```

We start with the ❶ global configuration for BGP, including flap dampening. Then we have the ❷ routes the router will announce, and we indicate that they're reachable via ❸ static routes. The router knows the IP address of two peers, ❹ ISP A and ❺ ISP B, and it has route maps for each.

Outside the BGP configuration, we have a ❻ static route for the block we wish to announce, and a matching ❼ access list so that we can allow BGP sessions to announce this block.

Finally, we have route maps for both ❽ ISP A and ❾ ISP B, so that we can attach the access list to the BGP session. While the route maps are initially identical, they soon may not be, so they should be separate.

Managing BGP

View BGP activity with the show ip bgp commands. A plain show ip bgp will display every route your router knows about via BGP, which is hundreds of thousands of lines of output. Most people consider this less than useful. Assorted subcommands break this down into palatable chunks, the most commonly used of which is sho ip bgp summary. The BGP summary is a nice snapshot of the router's BGP information, including memory usage, routes available, flapping routes, and so on, and ends with a very useful line for each BGP peer.

```
router# sho ip b s
BGP router identifier 10.1.8.6, local AS number 100
...
Neighbor        V    AS MsgRcvd MsgSent    TblVer  InQ OutQ Up/Down  State/PfxRcd
❶10.1.8.5       4 ❷200 1486094   19609    155050 ❸0    0 ❹1w6d      ❺132868
 172.16.0.2     4  300 ❻510754   19621 ❼155050   0    0  1w1d       115598
router#
```

By far, the most interesting columns are Neighbor and AS, which allow you to identify a peer by either ❶ IP address or ❷ ASN. The ❸ InQ and OutQ columns show how many messages from or to that peer remain to be processed, respectively. ❹ Up/Down shows how long the current BGP session has been established. Finally, during normal operation, the ❺ State/ PfxRcd column shows the number of route announcements that your router has received from that peer. If the BGP session has just been started or is having problems, this entry will display a word describing the state of the BGP session. An Active session has just been started, and your router is waiting for the other router to begin communication. An OpenSent or OpenConfirm status indicates that your router is negotiating with the peer to establish a connection. The Established state means that the routers are now exchanging routing information.

The remaining columns are less useful in day-to-day work, but might be important when troubleshooting. The ❻ MsgRcvd and MsgSent columns tell you how often you have received and transmitted BGP messages. ❼ TblVer gives the latest version of the BGP table that you've transmitted to your peers. Most of the time, you will only need these when you're on the phone with Cisco support.

Viewing Routes

The most frequently asked question when running BGP is, "Which circuit are we using to reach such-and-such website?"[3] That's simple with the show ip route command, specifying the IP address you're interested in.

---

[3] Actually, the most frequently asked question seems to be, "What do you mean, BGP doesn't load balance?" This is merely the most frequently asked *useful* question.

```
router# sho ip route 10.3.5.8
Routing entry for ❶10.3.0.0/16, supernet
  Known via "❷bgp 200", distance 20, metric 0
  Tag 200, type external
  Last update from 172.16.0.2 ❸00:09:37 ago
  Routing Descriptor Blocks:
  * 172.16.0.2, from 172.16.0.2, 00:09:37 ago
      Route metric is 0, traffic share count is 1
      ❹AS Hops 1
router#
```

The IP address we're interested in is ❶ announced as part of a /16 block. We get the route from our peer at ❷ AS200. This route was updated from our peer ❸ 9 minutes and 37 seconds ago. Finally, to reach this destination we need to pass through ❹ one autonomous system.

After you know which path your packets will take, you might want to know *why* they're taking that path. (Some people are never satisfied, after all!) You can examine the BGP information for a particular IP address with the show ip bgp command.

```
router# sho ip b 10.3.5.8
BGP routing table entry for 10.3.0/16, version 1912659
Paths: (❶2 available, best #1, table Default-IP-Routing-Table)
❷Not advertised to any peer
❸200
❹  172.16.0.2 from 172.16.0.2 (172.16.1.3)
      Origin IGP, metric 0, localpref 100, valid, external,
❺best
❻  300 400 700 200
    10.1.8.5 from 10.1.8.5 (10.1.2.87)
      Origin IGP, localpref 100, valid, external
router#
```

Our router has ❶ two paths to this IP address, which makes sense—you have two Internet connections, after all!

We are ❷ not re-advertising this route to our peers, which is good—if you're advertising routes from one peer to another, you're telling the peer that you can provide access to these IP addresses. Redistributing routes learned via BGP to your ISPs would mean that you're paying your ISP for the privilege of carrying the ISP's traffic for them. With proper BGP setup, you should never re-advertise the routes you learn from your peers. (That's why we used redistribute static earlier; with this set, your router will only announce the networks it knows about via static routes to your peers.)

From ❸ AS200, we reach the destination IP address via an AS path of 200. This means that the target IP is part of AS200. You would expect that AS200 has the best path to reach this destination. BGP knows the ❹ next IP address to send the packets to, the provider's side of the circuit going to AS200. It's figured out that this route is the ❺ best it has.

❻ Via AS300, we reach the destination IP address via an AS path of 300 400 700 200. In other words, the packets will have to go through four autonomous systems. This is probably longer than the route directly through AS200, so we don't want to take it.

Resetting BGP

BGP runs almost perfectly, and rarely has any problems at all. I've let routers run for months without changing their BGP configurations. On occasion you might find that your routing is behaving oddly; perhaps all of your traffic is running over one circuit, indicating that the other peer is not sending you any routes. Or perhaps the peer isn't receiving your route announcements, and so all of your incoming traffic is arriving via the other ISPs. One common step in these circumstances is to reset the BGP session, forcing your router and the peer to dump everything that they've previously agreed on, re-initialize the connection, and completely reload the routing table. The command for this is `clear ip bgp` followed by the neighbor's IP address.

```
router# clear ip bgp 172.16.0.2
router#
```

This should not be done lightly! Existing connections to the Internet may hang momentarily or even terminate. The router's CPU utilization will climb dramatically as the routes are cleared and all the new BGP information is received from the peer. If you have an older or smaller router, you can expect your terminal window to be almost useless.

On a more serious note, the rest of the world will see that your routes have just "flapped"; they've been withdrawn from that peer, and suddenly reappear. If you do this several times in quick succession, other autonomous systems will "dampen" your route announcements due to flap. They will ignore your route updates, and they may ignore routes to your network entirely until you can stop bouncing up and down. This is a necessary part of BGP; sudden withdrawals and insertions of a particular route can cause smaller routers to overload and crash. It's generally assumed that route flap is due to circuit or hardware problems, not someone repeatedly resetting their BGP session. A BGP reset can be thought of as the computer equivalent of dropping a cinderblock on your foot—you won't be able to do much beside hop around on one foot and think about what you've done for a few minutes. Routers assume that even if you have a good reason for doing it once, you're smart enough to not keep on doing it.[4]

Having said that, you can clear all of your BGP sessions simultaneously by using an asterisk instead of an IP address. All of the warnings above apply even more strongly for such mass BGP resets.

If your BGP problems persist, contact the ISP that is showing the odd behavior and ask who has been playing with the router configuration.

NOTE *Monitoring Router Traffic*
How are you supposed to know how your traffic is flowing over each circuit? Although you have several options I highly recommend using the free tool MRTG (http://www.mrtg.org) to perform basic router monitoring. MRTG will tell you how much traffic is going in and out each circuit, and it can be expanded to track how much memory and CPU time your router is using. I don't know how anyone can possibly manage a router without using MRTG or an equivalent tool.

Load Balancing BGP

If you were paying attention, you probably caught the emphatic bit earlier about how BGP is not a load-balancing protocol and find the title of this section inexplicable. BGP does not perform load balancing, but you can do some manual tricks that will allow you to adjust usage of your Internet circuits. You can also purchase products that will add load balancing to BGP or perform pseudo load balancing via DNS or NAT, or perform other unrelated tricks. Without purchasing additional equipment, however, you can use the BGP protocol against itself to perform crude load adjustments. By judiciously adding AS "hops" to the routes you receive and offer, you can increase the distance that the BGP algorithm sees to routes from different network areas.

---

[4] This may be the most fundamental difference between computers and human beings.

Before you can adjust your router's traffic flow, you must know how much traffic goes over your circuits on a long-term basis. I previously suggested MRTG (http://www.mrtg.org) for traffic measurement, and I suggest it even more strongly here. If you're reading this without setting up a traffic measurement tool, you may not have shot yourself in the foot yet, but you have loaded the gun and started eyeing your big toe.

Look at your traffic throughput on each provider. Frequently, your router will choose to transmit outbound traffic to one provider more often than the other. It's quite common to see a small office with two T1 circuits using one circuit ten times more than the other. When one circuit is using 1.0Mb/second, the other might only be using 0.1Mb/second. This is fine if your bandwidth usage is low, but if your more popular circuit fills up, you'll only be using 0.15Mb/second on your less popular circuit. This would give you network usage of about 1.6Mb/second, or only slightly more than half your available bandwidth. Worse, network requests sent out over the popular circuit will return very, very slowly. Similarly, if most of your traffic arrives over one circuit, you may find that one circuit is choked with inbound requests while your alternate circuit is empty.

If you go look at the routes in your router for destinations that are being reached over the slow circuit, you'll see that they are being sent that way because they have the shortest AS path. For example, assume that your router prefers to send traffic over one circuit in heavy preference over the other. Pick some random site that is always reached via one provider and check its BGP information. Here, we've chosen to check the BGP information on the system 192.1.120.84.

```
router# sho ip b 192.1.120.84
BGP routing table entry for 192.1.120.0/24, version 4521114
Paths: (2 available, ❶best #1, table Default-IP-Routing-Table)
  Not advertised to any peer
  ❷300 400
    172.16.0.2 from 172.16.0.2 (129.250.61.128)
      Origin IGP, metric 0, localpref 100, valid, external, best
      Community: 190972324 190973904 190974904
  ❸200 600 500
    10.1.8.5 from 10.1.8.5 (10.1.8.23)
      Origin IGP, localpref 100, valid, external
router#
```

This first route is across ❷ two autonomous systems, 300 and 400. The second route traverses ❸ three autonomous systems,

200, 600, and 500. The first route uses fewer autonomous systems, so it is ❶ preferred.

In this common unequal-use situation, one provider consistently offers a shorter AS path to other networks than the other. This is not at all uncommon, and is not a symptom that one network is "better connected" than another; in fact, it may be that the provider with the higher AS count has faster connections than the other! Now that you understand the problem, the solution is obvious: make the AS path of the more heavily used peer longer, so that your router will choose it less often. In this example, we want to increase the path length of routes we receive from AS300. You can adjust path length via AS path by prepending (adding) additional AS numbers in front of a peer.

Here is the snippet of BGP configuration that we must alter and its current route maps.

```
router bgp 100
 neighbor 172.16.0.2 remote-as 300❶
 neighbor 172.16.0.2 route-map ispB-out ❷out
route-map ispB-out❸
 match ip address 130
```

Our ❶ AS300 peering session currently has only one route map, and it is applied to ❷ outbound announcements. If we wanted to alter our announcements to this peer, we could edit the existing ❸ route map, but we want to alter the incoming announcements from this peer, so we need a new route map.

```
router# conf t
router(config)# router bgp 100
router(config-route)# neighbor 172.16.0.2 route-map ❶ispB-in ❷in
router(config-route)# ^Z
```

Here, we tell the BGP session to use a new route map for ISP B, called ❶ ispB-in. This new route map is applied only to ❷ incoming announcements.

```
router# conf t
router(config)# route map ❶ispB-in permit 10
router(config-route)# set ❷as-path ❸prepend ❹300 300
```

This creates the ispB-in route map. Every announcement that arrives over it will have its ❷ AS path extended by ❸ prepending ❹ two 300s to it.

After you make this change and save your work, make the new route map take effect by clearing this peer's BGP session.

```
router# clear ip bgp 172.16.0.2
```

When you have reset the BGP session, recheck your test routes.
The output will have a few minor, but important, changes.
Specifically, the AS path from AS300 will now have two extra
300s in front of it, much like this:

```
300 300 300 400
```

This will make the other AS path appear shorter and thus make
it preferable for this route.

Do not be too quick with AS path prepending. While we
added two AS hops in this example, it is best to add a single AS
hop to a peer at a time to see how it affects performance. If
necessary, you can add additional hops later. (You do have
MRTG running to display the effects of this every few minutes,
correct?)

If your incoming traffic is biased toward one peer or
another, change your outgoing announcements to balance
those. The important thing to remember here is that you must
prepend your own AS number to outbound announcements
instead of your peer's. You would be quite annoyed if someone
else started using your AS number, and you can expect that your
peers feel the same about theirs.

The nice thing here is that you already have outbound
route maps. To add an AS path prepend, simply edit the
existing map to add the line for AS path prepending.

```
router# conf t
router(config)# route map ❶ispB-out permit 10
router(config-route)# ❷set as-path prepend 100
```

Our BGP configuration already references the ispB-out route
map, so we don't have to touch the BGP configuration at all.
Just go into configure mode and edit the ❶ existing route map
to add the ❷ AS prepending rule. You still must clear the BGP
session with this peer to make the change take effect, however.

Propagation of BGP Updates

Now that you know enough about BGP to be dangerous,
you should know that BGP announcements may take up to
20 minutes to be visible throughout the world. Although your
peers should pick them up quickly, you can't expect that everyone everywhere is so well connected to you. After changing your

BGP setup, wait at least 20 minutes to see what the real effects are before making another change. This will also help reduce the risk of being marked as a flapping BGP source and black-holing yourself off the Internet.

If you want to see how your BGP announcements are being viewed by the outside world, search the Internet for a "BGP Looking Glass." These are web pages that allow you to query routers for BGP information. By asking remote routers for BGP information on your block of IP addresses, you can see what announcements they are seeing and how other people view your network. If you are having a problem with BGP config-uration, you can use several looking glasses to determine who can see your routes and who cannot, and thereby identify the scope of the problem. This information can also help you to identify problems such as one of your peers not propagating your announcements beyond their network or altering your announcements in some way.

Hot Standby Router Protocol

After you have BGP up and running, the next obvious question is, "What do we do if the router itself fails?" While Cisco routers are generally reliable, even the best hardware sometimes lets the magic smoke escape and transforms into a shiny metal paperweight. Cisco supports the Hot Standby Router Protocol (HSRP) to provide live failover between routers in this even-tuality. You can build a "pool" of independent Cisco devices that will take over some functions of a failed router; not all of the functions are covered, but enough are so that your users will not notice.

What Is HSRP?

HSRP lets multiple routers provide a single IP address. This is most useful for your default gateway on your Ethernet. All your computers know about the routers is that one of them had better have the default gateway of (for example) 192.168.0.1; they don't care which router has it, just that it's available. HSRP allows the routers to keep track of each other; when the router that has the default gateway disappears from the network, another router can automatically respond to requests for the default gateway's IP address. In this case, each router has its own unique IP address on its Ethernet interface, but might also have the default gateway as shown in Figure 7-2.

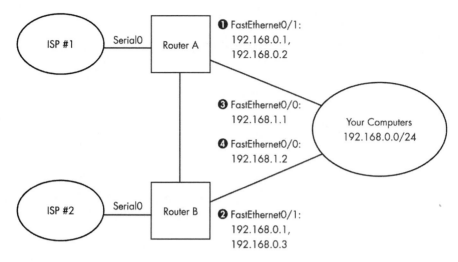

Figure 7-2: A typical HSRP setup

Router A has an ❶ Ethernet interface on the office network. This interface has the primary IP address of 192.168.0.2, but it can also host the IP address 192.168.0.1—the default gateway for your computers. If you want to log in to Router A, SSH to the address 192.168.0.2. Similarly, Router B also has an ❷ Ethernet interface on the office network and a unique IP address of 192.168.0.3, but it can also host the default gateway of 192.168.0.1. The routers settle between themselves which is the "default" default router, but when that router fails, the other will take over. In Cisco terminology, the IP address 192.168.0.1 is the *standby* address. (Other implementations commonly call this a Virtual IP, or VIP.)

Very basic configuration of this Ethernet interface is only a couple of lines.

```
router(config)# int faste0/0
router(config-if)# ip address 192.168.0.2 255.255.255.0
router(config-if)# ❶standby ❷1 ip 192.168.0.1
```

Apply the ❶ standby entry to both router configurations, and abruptly you'll be able to ping 192.168.0.1. Keep pinging that IP while you reboot routers, and you won't even see a single dropped packet—unless, of course, you turn both routers off at once!

A single router interface can support multiple HSRP standby IP addresses. Each has to be identified as a ❷ group. Use the group identifier in every configuration involving that particular standby IP.

Tuning HSRP

While the above will handle most of the work of live failover for most circumstances, you'll find that HSRP requires some fine-tuning to be truly transparent. The most commonly tweaked features are *preemption, interface tracking, delay,* and *authentication.*

Preemption

Preemption is where a particular interface declares itself to be in charge of the standby IP address and forces all others to relinquish their claims to that address. This means that a particular router defaults to supporting the HSRP, letting all others only be backups. This is handled by assigning a priority to each interface that supports the standby IP, and letting the router with the highest priority claim it. By default, every router in a standby group has a priority of 100. To set a priority, use the keyword priority in the configuration.

```
router(config)# int faste0/0
router(config-if)# standby 1 ❶preempt
router(config-if)# standby 1 ❷priority 105
```

Start by allowing this router to ❶ demand to host the standby IP from lower-priority routers. If you use preemption, all routers in a standby group should have this entry. Then set this particular router to have a priority of ❷ 105.

Interface Tracking

It can be convenient to assign a single router to be the master of the standby group, if only so you know which router is in charge. (Network administrators, as a class, are not comfortable saying that "traffic goes into a cloud near our routers and magic things happen." They prefer statements such as, "Traffic *will* unquestionably go to Router A as long as A is running.") At times, your chosen router might not be a sensible choice. Look at Figure 7-2 again. Each of our routers has a single line to the Internet. If a router's Internet circuit goes down, it no longer makes sense for that router to be the standby master; traffic would go through an extra hop for no good reason. We can cause a router's HSRP priority to drop by using interface tracking. When your interface being tracked goes down, the HSRP priority automatically decreases.

```
router(config)# int faste0/0
router(config-if)# standby 1 ❶track ❷Serial0
```

The standby IP number 1 is ❶ monitoring the interface ❷ Serial0. When Serial0 goes down, it will automatically decrease its priority by 10. If this router's priority has been set to 105, it will become 95. Because the other router has the default priority of 100, it suddenly has higher priority and takes over as the standby IP.

HSRP Delay

When a router first boots, it takes a few seconds for it to get its bearings and start routing traffic. If the router uses BGP, those few seconds can be as long as a minute or two. HSRP, on the other hand, works quickly. If your preferred router takes over the standby IP address before it has a chance to sort out its BGP routing tables, traffic will stop flowing until the router is comfortable. To let your router get its feet properly under the table, you can assign a delay to HSRP failover.

Time how long it takes for your router to reassemble all of its BGP sessions and for the CPU to drop to only normally busy after you type `clear ip bgp *`. Round it up 10 or 15 seconds, just to allow time for the unexpected. That's how long your standby IP should wait before failing over.

```
router(config)# int faste0/0
router(config-if)# standby 1 preempt ❶delay ❷minimum ❸60
```

This router will ❶ wait a ❷ minimum of ❸ 60 seconds before taking over the standby IP address.

Authentication

It's quite unlikely that an intruder would break into your HSRP cluster. This would require a fair amount of talent and knowledge. If they managed to do so, however, the effects could be devastating. Imagine if an intruder funneled all network traffic through a packet analyzer illegally installed on one of your machines; they could capture usernames, passwords, credit card numbers, customer details, and so on. For that reason, using some basic authentication on your HSRP standby group is a good idea. HSRP uses a simple password for authentication. Any router that knows the password is permitted to participate in the HSRP group.

```
router(config)# int faste0/0
router(config-if)# standby 1 ❶authentication ❷PassWord
```

Here, we set standby group 1 to use a ❶ password of ❷ `PassWord`. It might not be the strongest authentication mechanism in the world, but it's far better than nothing.

Given these features, you should be able to tune HSRP to do almost anything you like. There's one more complication with router redundancy, however: routing.

BGP and HSRP

Take another look at Figure 7-2. We have Router A connected to ISP #1, and Router B connected to ISP #2. Both Router A and Router B are announcing their network addresses to their ISPs. Systems in the outside world will send their traffic to your network via their closest route. But with HSRP set up as we've discussed, your network will only use one outbound circuit at a time! Think about it; Router A only knows of routes it receives from ISP #1, so that's where it sends everything. If Router A is holding the default route, even traffic meant for ISP #2 will go out via ISP #1. This is inefficient, and it places a very real limitation on your bandwidth use. To actually use both ISPs for outbound traffic, you need to speak BGP between your routers.

In Figure 7-2, we show a pair of separate Ethernet interfaces for a connection between the two routers. Router A has the ❸ IP address of 192.168.1.1, while ❹ Router B has 192.168.1.2. Nothing else is on this network; I just use a crossover cable between the two routers.

NOTE   *Nugget of Wisdom*
Yes, you can speak BGP over the shared network where the rest of your traffic is passed around. This increases the amount of traffic on your main network, however, and slows down outbound traffic. A packet bound for ISP #2 will reach Router A and immediately be turned around and sent back across the same network it came from to Router B, dramatically increasing potential collisions on your local network. I've seen any number of weird problems from this, but feel free to try it if your routers have only one Ethernet interface.

BGP calculates its preferred routes by counting the number of AS hops to the destination IP address. One thing you don't want to have happen is for BGP to count the other router in your network as a penalty—presumably, bandwidth on your crossover cable is pretty much unlimited. (If it's not, you need a better crossover cable, a better router, or *serious* help!) You don't need to apply any sort of access list to the BGP session between your two routers, because you already do that on your peers. If your AS is number 100, the BGP session between the two would look like this:

```
router(config)# router bgp 100
router(config-router)# neighbor 192.168.1.1 neighbor-as 100
router(config-router)# neighbor 192.168.1.1 next-hop-self
```

Save your work, and suddenly your two routers will be speaking internal BGP and your internal traffic will be taking the best available route out of your network.

Testing HSRP

The easy way to test live failover is to unplug a router during the day and see who complains. I agree that this is the true test of failover, but it is best performed after hours with your network's monitoring system running at full tilt. You can check your router's HSRP behavior by using the sho standby command.

```
router#sho standby
FastEthernet0/0 - Group ❶1
  State is ❷Standby
    ❸1 state change, last state change 1w2d
  ❹Virtual IP address is 192.168.0.1
  Active virtual MAC address is 0000.0c07.ac01
    Local virtual MAC address is 0000.0c07.ac01 (default)
  Hello time 3 sec, hold time 10 sec
    Next hello sent in 2.648 secs
  ❺Authentication text "PassWord"
  ❻Preemption enabled, delay min 60 secs
  ❼Active router is 192.168.0.3, priority 105 (expires in 7.020 sec)
  Standby router is local
  ❽Priority 100 (configured 100)
  ❾  Track interface Serial0 state Up decrement 10
  IP redundancy name is "hsrp-Fa0/0-1" (default)
```

You'll see an entry like this for every HSRP ❶ group you have configured on your routers. While most people only have one HSRP group, you can have several.

What you probably care most about is the router's current status; is it in charge or not? This router is in a state of ❷ Standby, meaning that it's not hosting the standby IP. If this said Active, this router would be hosting the standby IP.

When debugging, it's nice to know ❸ how often the standby IP has moved and when it last moved. Just in case you forgot, it also shows the ❹ standby IP address and the ❺ authentication password.

We then proceed to the preemption information; this router has ❻ preemption on, and will wait at least 60 seconds before preempting another router. You'll also see ❼ which router is currently the active router; while this is obvious in a group of two routers, it can be very helpful if you have a few routers in the standby group.

Finally, you can see the router's ❽ current priority and the ❾ state of interfaces being tracked.

When you have BGP and HSRP, you're about as redundant as you can get. The only things that can take your network out now are telco outages, power outages, and large-scale meteor strikes. (OK, fine; small but well-targeted meteor strikes would also suffice.) Those can all be dealt with, but they're a topic for other books.

8

LOGINS, AUTHENTICATION, AND REMOTE ACCESS

Restricting access to your router's configuration and controls is an important part of network management. While it's important to get the router up and running, you don't want just anyone to be able to access your equipment and reconfigure it! It's important to understand how your router can be accessed, how to set passwords and create individual usernames, and how to offer and control access over the network via telnet or SSH.

Lines

Near the end of your router's configuration, you'll see entries like line vty 0 4 and line con 0. These lines are the available methods of getting a command line prompt on your router, and each can be configured separately. A standard Cisco device has three types of line: con, aux, and vty.

The *con* (or console) port is what we've been using to connect to the system. While it's entirely possible to reconfigure this port, it's generally a bad idea. You can set the console to require a password to log in, for example, or you might have it run at a higher speed for better interactive response. If you need a physical console port with nonstandard behavior, use the *aux* (or auxiliary) port. That's what it's there for.

The *vty* lines, or virtual terminals, are logical lines used for access over the network. Telnet and SSH connections into the router are directed to a virtual terminal. These lines have no physical hardware; they are strictly a software interface. (That's why they're called "virtual.") These lines may cause the most concern and require the most attention; while a locked door can control access to the con and aux ports, the whole point of remote network access is that you can access your router from anywhere.

Each router supports a different number of lines. The easy way to identify the lines is with the show line command.

```
router#show line
  Tty  Typ   Tx/Rx       A  Modem  Roty  AccO  AccI  Uses  Noise  Overruns  Int
    0  CTY❶                -    -     -     -     -     0     0     0/0       -
  129  AUX❷  9600/9600     -    -     -     -     -     0     0     0/0       -
* 130  VTY❸                -    -     -     -     -    18❹    0     0/0       -
  131  VTY                 -    -     -     -     -     6     0     0/0       -
  132  VTY                 -    -     -     -     -     3     0     0/0       -
  133  VTY                 -    -     -     -     -     2     0     0/0       -
  134  VTY❺                -    -     -     -     -     0     0     0/0       -
```

Here, we see that this particular router has a single ❶ console, a single ❷ aux port, and five virtual terminals numbered ❸ 130 through ❺ 134. While most of the rest of the information is not normally useful, sometimes it's nice to see ❹ how many times a particular terminal has been accessed.

While you can do all sorts of configuration on these ports, the most important features are those related to passwords and access methods. Let's look at a sample configuration and see what we can learn.

```
line con 0❶
 ❷password 7 02310042864A2C295D43D1
line aux 0❸
 password 7 02310042864A2C295D43D1
line ❹vty ❺0 ❻4
 ❼login local
 ❽transport input telnet ssh
```

The first entry is the ❶ console port. Like all real computer devices, Cisco numbers ports beginning with zero. This console port has a ❷ password on it; even if you hook up a serial cable and fire up HyperTerminal, you'll have to enter a password. This may be necessary if your router is physically insecure, such as in a shared colocation center. (It may also be necessary if your company has staff that like to wander into places they aren't supposed to.) If your router is correctly configured, the actual password is stored in encrypted form.

The ❸ aux port is also numbered 0 and has a password. While the password for both the console and aux ports are encrypted, you can see that they are identical.

Last, we have the ❹ virtual terminals. This system has five configured virtual terminals, numbered ❺ 0 through ❻ 4. The ❼ login local keyword means that this router has a list of usernames and passwords stored on the local machine, and that whenever a login request arrives over the network, the router should use this list. The ❽ transport line indicates what methods can be used to access the virtual terminals; in this case, acceptable inputs are telnet and SSH.

Unconfigured virtual terminals cannot be used; if we configured only virtual ports 0 and 1, the router would only support two simultaneous remote login sessions. While this might not seem like a problem, at times it's nice to have multiple router command prompts open simultaneously so that you can, say, keep watching your BGP sessions in one window and make changes in another. I've found myself at times with all four virtual terminals open on my single desktop when I'm trying to debug a particularly annoying problem.

How can you set all this up? Well, let's find out.

Passwords

A password is the simplest authentication method a Cisco router can use, but it's effective enough for most networks. If you have dozens of routers, you may want to consider a solution such as

RAIDUS or TACACS+, but that really is overkill for most environments. By default, routers do not require passwords, but also by default, you cannot access the router over the network, so in order to get a command prompt on the router, you would need to have physical access. Cisco assumes that if you know enough to enable network access, you will be able to set up basic passwords.

Before implementing passwords on your router, make certain that the password encryption service is activated. By default, routers store passwords in their configuration in *unencrypted* format. This means that anyone who can view the router's configuration can see the router's passwords! While it's true that you already have to have privileged mode access to view a running router's configuration, that doesn't protect backup copies of your configuration stored elsewhere. It also makes it almost impossible for someone who happens to be looking over your shoulder to *not* view the password, even if they want to be honest. To enable the password encryption service, just add

---

```
service password-encryption
```

---

to your configuration.

Now that nobody can get your passwords trivially, it's worth continuing. Standard Cisco devices offer three standard pass-words: the *front door, enable,* and *enable secret.* The front door password protects unprivileged EXEC mode access to the router. This means that you can look but not touch, as discussed earlier. Setting a front door password for a line is very simple. Here, we're setting a front door password on our aux port.

```
router# conf t❶
router(config)# line aux 0❷
router(config-line)# login❸
router(config-line)# password YourPassword❹
router(config-line)# ^Z
```

Start by ❶ entering configure mode, and then tell the router that you want to ❷ configure the line aux 0. Remember, your router configuration will tell you exactly what the line is called; if nothing else, you'll see a single line near the end of the configuration that says only line aux 0. You need to tell the router to ❸ use password checking on this port with the login option. Finally, enter the command password and ❹ your chosen password. Unlike more modern operating systems that provide you with shaded dialog boxes that hide your password as you change it, your password will actually appear on the command line here. Be certain that nobody's looking over your shoulder when you set or change the password!

After you've set a password, you'll see an entry for it in the router configuration.

```
line aux 0
  password ❶7 ❷053C02162C006D01080856
  login
```

This looks an awful lot like what you typed, but ❷ the password has been hashed. Another thing to note is the ❶ 7 between the word password and the password string. The 7 tells the router that the password has been hashed, and that the string 053C02162C006D01080856 isn't the actual password.

One thing to remember is that these front door passwords are configured on a line-by-line basis. You can have one password for your console port, another for the aux port, and yet another for your virtual terminals. Setting different passwords on different ports is a wonderful way to confuse yourself.

The *enable* password protects access to privileged EXEC mode. The old method of Cisco access control was to give lower-level support techs the front door password but restrict the enable mode to higher-level techs. Unfortunately, Cisco created its own encryption algorithm to keep the password secure. This algorithm is badly flawed. You should not have an enable password on your Cisco devices, because anyone who gets your configuration can trivially reverse engineer the enable password from the scrambled hash.[1] To fix this, Cisco introduced a second privileged EXEC protection, the *enable secret*, and protected it with the cryptographically sound MD5 hash. Setting an enable secret, and disabling the enable password, is much like setting a front door password. Unlike the front door passwords, which can be different for each line, the enable passwords work globally.

```
router# ❶conf t
router(config)# ❷enable secret YourSecretPassword
router(config)# ❸no enable password
```

---

[1] This happens more frequently than you might think. Whenever a vendor says that it has invented its own proprietary, highly secure encryption techniques, run. Run quickly. While the security of "open code" versus "closed code" may be debatable, the security of "open crypto" versus "closed crypto" most certainly is not.

When you're in ❶ standard configure mode, the command ❷ `enable secret` and a password string will set the enable secret. You don't want any sort of easily retrievable password on any system, so be sure to ❸ disable the old-fashioned enable password.

These passwords will provide some basic protection to your system. You can also change passwords at any time with exactly the same commands you used to set them in the first place.

Usernames

While global passwords are sufficient to protect your router from the most ignorant network intruders, you will probably want to secure the remote command-line access to the router. Cisco provides secure shell (SSH) server for secure remote administration. SSH requires that each user have a username. In large networks, you can use usernames to assign different users different privilege levels on each router as required.

Each user needs a username, a password, and a privilege level. Privilege levels range from 1 (unprivileged EXEC) to 15 (privileged EXEC). To create a username, just go into configure mode and enter all the information.

```
router(config)# username ❶mwlucas privilege ❷15 password ❸mwlucas-password
router(config)# username ❹kgball privilege ❺1 password kgball-password
```

The first username we're creating is ❶ mwlucas. This user has a ❷ privilege level of 15, meaning that he is in enable mode when he logs in. While you give this user's ❸ password on the command line when you're creating him, it will be hashed and appear scrambled when you view the configuration later.

The second username we're creating is ❹ kgball. The only different thing about him is that he is at ❺ privilege level 1. He can look at everything but cannot make any changes, exactly as if he only had the front door password.

While you can assign particular privilege levels to different commands, and then assign each user a privilege level commensurate with their duties and abilities, in most small networks two privilege levels are quite sufficient.

Making Lines Check Usernames

After you have assigned usernames and passwords, you need to tell the router's lines to use them. Adding the `login local` line to a line will tell the router to check incoming connection requests against the local users database. For example, to make the console check usernames you would just do this:

```
router# conf t
router(config)# line con 0
router(config-line)# login local
```

You can mix and match different authentication methods on different lines. By setting login local on the vty lines and login on the con port, you require a username and password for remote access but the standard front door password for the console. This provides more than enough possible combinations for you to completely lock yourself out of the system.

Remote Router Access

Cisco routers support a variety of methods for administration over the network. The most common methods of accessing a router are telnet and SSH.

Telnet was the standard method to get a command prompt on a remote system for many, many years. Unfortunately, everything sent over telnet is unencrypted. For twenty-odd years, this didn't matter a great deal, but these days the Internet is much less friendly. A hostile Internet user between your computer and your router can capture your router passwords and do anything they like to your router. If you must use telnet, be certain you only use it from a trusted network local to the router and not over the public Internet. Both Unix and Windows include a command-line telnet client. If at all possible, use SSH instead of telnet.

SSH, or Secure Shell, is the modern replacement for telnet. All communications between client and server are encrypted, so that same hostile user cannot capture any useful information. While all modern Unix versions include an SSH client, Windows users will need to get an add-on SSH client. Many clients are available from the Internet, but one of the most commonly recommended is puTTY. A Google search will take you directly to any number of download sites.

Many Cisco routers support other configuration methods, such as a web interface. Like telnet, any information you transmit is sent over the network unencrypted, and anyone who knows how to can capture it and gain unrestricted access to your router. A router's web interface is frequently not as flexible as the command line. Between the two, there is little to recommend the web interface.

Enabling Telnet

To use telnet, the router must have a password set on the vty
lines, or local usernames and passwords that the vty lines can be
told to authenticate against. If you have already set a password
on the lines, just adding the transport input telnet configuration
option to the vty line configuration will turn on telnet.

```
line vty 0 4
❶password 7 0231004206EA2C295D4848
 transport input telnet
```

If a ❶ password is not set on the vty lines, the router will reject
all attempts to connect via telnet. Otherwise, telnet will just start
working with this simple configuration.

If you want to use local usernames, skip assigning a password on the vty lines. Just be certain to add the option login
local to the vty line configuration in addition to the transport
input telnet line.

```
router# conf t
router(config)# line vty 0 4
router(config-line)# login local
router(config-line)# transport input telnet
```

This tells the router to authenticate incoming telnet requests
against the local usernames list.

Enabling SSH

The SSH protocol might be more secure than telnet, but its
complexity leads to its needing more configuration than telnet.
Much of this configuration is stuff that is nice to have on a
router anyway, so it shouldn't be a burden.

To use SSH, the router must have an IOS version that
supports SSH. Generally speaking, the Enterprise and DES
feature sets include SSH support. If your router doesn't have an
IOS version that supports SSH, get a new one from Cisco. Feel
free to open a request with Cisco's Technical Assistance Center,
requesting help in selecting an IOS version, or if you're brave,
you can wander through the Cisco website and use its IOS
selection tool. Also go back and read Chapter 6 carefully.

The router must have user accounts on the virtual terminals
instead of generic passwords, as discussed earlier this chapter.
When you have those, however, your router must know its
hostname and its domain name.

```
router# conf t
router(config)# hostname ❶router.blackhelicopters.org
router(config)# ip domain-name ❷blackhelicopters.org
```

This particular machine has the hostname ❶ router.blackheli-
copters.org and is part of the domain ❷ blackhelicopters.org.
While you might expect that a router could determine its
domain name from the hostname, if you have fourth- and fifth-
level domains, this gets harder to do than it sounds. After you
have these basics set, you can finish configuring SSH. One easy
way to determine if your current IOS version supports SSH is
to run these commands. If the router doesn't recognize them,
your IOS doesn't support SSH, and you need to change to a
different one.

```
router(config)# crypto key generate rsa❶
router(config)# ip ssh ❷timeout ❸60
router(config)# ip ssh ❹authentication-retries ❺3
router(config)# line vty 0 4❻
router(config-line)# transport input ssh❼
```

After you have the hostname and domain name set, ❶ generate
an RSA cryptographic key for your router. An RSA cryptographic key is a pair of very large numbers that your router uses
as a key to prove its identity to SSH clients. This key will not
show up in your router's configuration file; it's stored
separately.

SSH has two other options that you can set; the ❷ number
of seconds that the router will leave an idle SSH connection up
before closing it, and the ❹ number of tries an incoming SSH
connection has to enter a correct password. In this case, the
router will leave SSH connections open for ❸ 60 seconds and
give users ❺ three chances to enter the correct password.

Finally, we need to ❻ configure the virtual terminals and
tell the router that ❼ SSH is the incoming transport method
that it should accept. Of course, we also have to have the login
local statement so that the network will authenticate against the
usernames and passwords stored on the router.

Now you can securely access your router from anywhere in
the world. Let's go on to look at some other features offered by
Cisco to make your router a real participant in your network
instead of a mysterious gray box.

9

CISCO NETWORK SERVICES

If you've done everything in this book so far, your router should be fully functional and quickly processing packets to and from your network in exactly the manner you desire. In addition to simply forwarding packets, however, Cisco routers support many additional network protocols that can work well to integrate the router into your network services and network management systems. These include things such as Network Time Protocol, system logging, and SNMP.

As many of these services make use of timestamps, we'll start by making your router's idea of the current date and time bear some resemblance to reality.

NTP

If you're relying on system logs to identify problems (as opposed to traditional troubleshooting methods such as "blind guesswork"), having your logs properly timestamped can make the difference between useful and useless records. Network management systems often use a system's reported timestamp to record events. In the event someone breaks into your network and you have to involve law enforcement, inaccurate system time will effectively invalidate your records and your logs in the eyes of the legal system. While all of these combine to make network time important, maintaining synchronized network time across a variety of operating systems can be an annoyance. Cisco routers support Network Time Protocol (NTP), which is supported by all major operating system vendors and is the industry standard.

Basics of NTP

NTP allows a group of networked hosts to agree on the time, within a few milliseconds. The protocol works with two conflicting assumptions. First, some systems have very accurate clocks, and the system owners wish to provide others access to those clocks. Second, those same hosts that want to provide a public service of accurate time do not wish to be flooded by every possible client in the world. The NTP protocol allows one or two local servers to get accurate time from big global time servers, and then redistribute that correct time to other clients on the network. The systems with extremely accurate clocks are called Tier 1 NTP servers. Those systems that are allowed to pull time directly from Tier 1 NTP servers systems and redistribute it to clients are called Tier 2 NTP servers.

It is possible to configure your router to pull time directly from one of the big Tier 1 or Tier 2 NTP servers, but it's best to have a local NTP server. Generally speaking, this server will read time from two or three different Tier 2 NTP servers and allow other local systems to get their time from it. This reduces load on the Tier 2 servers and makes NTP easier for you to maintain. The Tier 1 and 2 time servers change their names or IP addresses on occasion, so it's simpler to update your configuration on a single local server than on every client on the network. Check your operating system documentation for details on how to provide time services to clients.

Configuring NTP

Enabling NTP on your router is as simple as telling the router the IP address of the local NTP server. Although one NTP server will suffice, if you have multiple servers, enter each in a separate configuration statement.

```
router(config)# ntp server 192.168.5.8
router(config)# ntp server 192.168.3.8
```

Wall clock time isn't the same throughout the world. By default, NTP distributes time in the Coordinated Universal Time (UTC) time zone, the modern successor to the old Greenwich Mean Time. Even if your clock is completely accurate, it's not necessarily convenient for your logs to have timestamps local to Europe. After you configure a time zone, your router will know exactly what sort of timestamp you'd like to have. A time zone is easily configured with the clock option.

```
router(config)# clock timezone ❶est ❷-5
router(config)# clock ❸summer-time ❹edt ❺recurring
```

To set the router's time zone, you need to know the ❶ name of the time zone. You probably know the name of your local time zone; if not, ask someone who spends a little less time with computers and a little more with other people. You also have to know ❷ how many hours this time zone is different from UTC. This is slightly obscure, but you can find any number of charts on the Internet that will give you this information.

Many parts of the world also observe Daylight Saving Time (DST), and your router can too. Cisco recognizes this as ❸ summer-time. To set DST, you need to know the ❹ name of your time zone during the summer. Finally, if you want your router to automatically change its clock with the changing of the time, use the ❺ recurring keyword.

Checking NTP

Your router may need a few moments to synchronize its clock with your NTP servers. If you want to make sure that your router is correctly performing NTP operations, you can check with the command sho ntp status.

```
router# sho ntp status
Clock is ❶synchronized, stratum 4, reference is ❷192.168.5.8
nominal freq is 250.0000 Hz, actual freq is 249.9991 Hz, precision is 2**24
reference time is C48A754E.88C5D76C (❸06:45:34.534 edt Mon Jun 28 2004)
clock offset is ❹-0.4631 msec, root delay is 65.75 msec
root dispersion is 53.45 msec, peer dispersion is 6.85 msec
```

This command displays more than you could possibly want to know about your router's clock behavior, but you can see that the router believes it has ❶ synchronized its clock with that of a ❷ particular NTP server. You can also see what ❸ time the router thinks it is. This should be accurate, because NTP deals with margins of error on the order of ❹ milliseconds.

You now have accurate time—congratulations! Now, let's set up a place to record all these timestamps, and maybe even some data with them.

Router Logging

A router knows when the equipment attached to it changes, when it has problems, and when people change its configuration. When you make changes to your router via the console, or if a circuit has a problem, you'll probably notice messages such as

```
%LINEPROTO-5-UPDOWN: Line protocol on Interface Serial3/1, changed state to down
```

By default, these messages are dumped onto the console so that the administrator can figure out what is happening. While this is nice, if you're not staring at the console 24 hours a day, it's less than helpful. While the router can store logging messages locally, it can also send these messages to another system for safekeeping. We'll start with the local logs and proceed to the more advanced remote logs.

Local Logging

The router can store a few messages locally, which allows you to check recent events on the systems. To use this system, you have to decide what level of logging you would like. Cisco follows the syslog standards for logging levels that have eight degrees of severity.

The *level* is an indication of the importance or severity of an individual message. Some messages are purely informational or contain# only debugging information, while other messages (such as the "circuit down" example above) are clearly quite important. The levels are, in order of increasing importance:

debugging   for debugging only

informational   general informational messages

notifications   events that may require special handling, but are not errors

warnings   minor errors

errors   real errors

critical   critical errors

alerts   errors that require immediate corrective action

emergencies   the router is now inoperable

When you specify a particular level, the router will log all messages of that severity level or higher. For example, if you specify that you want to log "info" level messages, the router will record all messages of the levels informational, notifications, warnings, errors, critical, alerts, or emergencies. Configuring basic logging requires only a couple of lines of code.

```
router# conf t
router(config)# service ❶log ❷timestamps ❸datetime ❹localtime
router(config)# ❺logging ❻history ❼debugging
```

Start by telling the router to provide basic ❶ logging services as well as ❸ dated ❷ timestamps in the ❹ local time. When you have that, you can tell the router to ❺ perform logging, keeping the ❻ history on the local system. End with the ❼ lowest level of severity of messages you wish to record.

You can view the log entries with the show logging command. This command will display a few lines of information about the logging configuration and then give the actual log entries.

```
router# show logging
...
Log Buffer (8192 bytes):

*Jun 29 10:17:46.079: %LINK-3-UPDOWN: Interface FastEthernet0/1,
changed state to up
*Jun 29 10:17:46.079: %LINK-3-UPDOWN: Interface FastEthernet0/0,
changed state to up
```

The important thing to remember is that the amount of space on the router for log messages is strictly limited and varies between different routers. If you want to keep more log messages, you must use syslog.

Syslog Basics

The *syslog* protocol requires a separate server to receive the messages from the router (and any other network devices that speak the syslog protocol). The server runs a syslog daemon, or *syslogd*. Syslogd has been integrated into all sorts of Unix-like operating systems for many, many years, and Microsoft server operating systems have quite a few syslogd implementations (both commercial and free). Syslog daemons are very small and have low impact on even modest systems, and I recommend using whichever version is most convenient for your environment. While the configuration of syslog daemons varies widely between programs, the protocol basics are unchanged. Syslog uses the same severity levels as local logging, but also uses a *facility* to label messages.

A facility is category provided by the syslog daemon for a group of programs to log to the same place. For example, the syslog facility called ftp is intended for FTP server log messages, as well as messages from related programs such as TFTP and SFTP servers. The daemon facility is intended for miscellaneous system daemons that require logging but don't really rate their own facility. In addition to a couple of dozen defined facilities much like these, a syslog daemon also has eight local facilities called local0 through local7 specifically for use by local systems administrators. Any one of these local categories is appropriate for your router messages; just pick one. The router will use any facility that you choose.

I recommend logging everything that the router produces; Cisco logs aren't very large, and when something breaks you'll want to be able to look at older logs. Once you have local logging configured, you only need to add a few lines to enable syslog logging.

```
router# conf t
router(config)# logging ❶trap ❷debugging
router(config)# logging ❸facility ❹local3
router(config)# logging ❺192.168.1.8
```

Logging ❶ traps are messages sent by the router. In this case, we want the router to transmit any log messages of ❷ debugging severity or greater to our syslog server (the severity levels are exactly the same as those used in local logging). The router tags each message with a particular ❸ facility we've set aside. In this case, we use the ❹ local3 facility. Finally, we tell the router the ❺ IP address of our logging server. Save your work, and every time the router generates a log entry it will send a message to your logging server.

When the syslog messages arrive at your logging server, the syslog daemon will check the facility and severity of each message and direct the message to the file you've chosen for those messages. This process happens extremely quickly; If your syslog server is correctly set up, you will start to see messages appear almost immediately.

SNMP

The most common glue to hold networks together is the Simple Network Management Protocol (SNMP). Many different products and tools use SNMP to gather and accumulate network and device performance information, and all of these include support for Cisco routers.

SNMP can be used in both read-only and read-write modes. Using read-write SNMP requires that your router be tightly secured. Because your router is usually the border device on your network, sitting outside your firewall, this is difficult. Read-only access is a much safer idea. (You can also use an access list to prevent random people from being able to query your router; check Cisco's website for details.)

A SNMP-enabled device uses a community name to provide basic security. This is much like a password; people that have the community ID can make SNMP queries of the router, while people without the community name cannot. Setting the community name is quite simple:

```
router# conf t
router(config)# ❶snmp-server ❷community ❸SendMichaelAllYourCash ❹RO
```

First, tell the router to ❶ fire up its SNMP server. You must set a ❷ community and pick ❸ some random jumble of characters to use as a community name. Finally, do not forget to set the community name to be ❹ read only! (While the router will use read-only SNMP by default, it's always a good idea to list this explicitly in case the system behavior should change with an IOS change.)

With SNMP support, logging, and timekeeping, you have the tools you need to successfully monitor and manage your router with the rest of your network management equipment. If you can do all this, as well as troubleshoot your own circuits and load balance your traffic with BGP, you're better off than almost all other Cisco users. Congratulations!

APPENDIX

IP ADDRESSES
AND NETMASKS

If you've been around the networking world for a while, you'll certainly recognize network blocks identified with *slash notation,* such as 10.0.0.0/8 or 209.69.8.0/23. If you know what these are, you can skip this appendix. Otherwise, read on.

What Is an IP Address?

An IP address is simply a 32-bit number assigned to particular network device. Rather than expressing that 32-bit number as a single number, IP addresses are usually shown broken up into four 8-bit numbers ranging from 0 to 255. It's much easier for our feeble brains to wrap around a number such as 192.168.0.1 than 11000000101010000000000000000001.

To really understand netmasks, it's important to remember that your IP addresses are really just a single long string of numbers.

A netmask is just a way of saying how many IP addresses you have in a particular block. The trick is that not all netmasks are legitimate, and you can't use just any netmask with any random IP address. If you've been kicking around the Internet for a while, you've probably seen the netmask 255.255.255.0. This was the standard for corporate networks for many years. This netmask means that you have 256 legitimate IP addresses in your network block. For example, if the IP address of your machine is 10.5.3.12 and it has a netmask of 255.255.255.0, you know that your local network has up to 255 other IP addresses on it. (It's rare that all of these would be used, and certain addresses would present difficulties, but it's within the possible.) This netmask is frequently called a *class C network*, although the term *class C* (and the other "class" network names) has been obsolete for about a decade now.

A netmask is simply the line between the network and the host IP address. The classic 255.255.255.0 netmask means that the IP number is fixed for the first 24 bits, and that you can change the last 8 bits. Confused yet? Let's look at an example. Suppose your ISP issues you the block of IP addresses 192.168.1.0 through 192.168.1.255, with a netmask of 255.255.255.0. The first 24 bits of the address are fixed, and you can do anything you want with the remaining 8 bits. Look at the netmask as a binary number, and it will start to make a whole lot more sense. In this example, any digit that is a 1 has been set by the ISP that issued you your IP addresses; any digit that is a 0 can be changed by the network administrator.

```
255.255.255.0 = 11111111.11111111.11111111.00000000
```

The first 24 bits are all 1s, meaning that you cannot change that part of the IP address on a machine on your local network. You can change the numbers that are in the "0" section of the netmask. The "192.168.1" part of the IP is all in the part of the netmask marked off by 1s, so you cannot change those numbers. The last chunk of the IP address, the part after the last period, is in the section marked off by 0s, so you can change this. The part of the IP address under the 1s in the netmask is called the *network address*. The remainder is called the *host address*.

Netmask size is measured by the number of 1s in the netmask. This netmask has 24 1s, so it is a 24-bit netmask or a /24 (pronounced "slash 24"). Your network block would be written as 192.168.1.0/24.

Here's the scary part: there is no reason why the boundary between the network number and the host number must lie on the convenient 8-bit boundary. The following is a perfectly legitimate netmask:

11111111.11111111.11111111.10000000

If you convert this from binary to decimal (a function on most calculators these days), you'll see that this is a netmask of 255.255.255.128. Don't let that scare you—it's a perfectly legitimate netmask, and it has 7 bits of addresses for your machines. That same calculator will show you that 2 to the power of 7 is 128, so you have 128 IP addresses for this network.

NOTE   *Unusable IP Addresses*
The first and last address in any block is unusable. You cannot assign a machine on a network with a netmask of 255.255.255.0 an IP ending in either .0 or .255.

Practical Netmasks

The end result of netmasks being in binary is that IP addresses are issued in blocks that are multiples of two. If you have 5 bits to play with, you'll have 32 ($2 \times 2 \times 2 \times 2 \times 2 = 32$) IP addresses on your network, and your netmask will be a /27 ($32 - 5 = 27$). If you have 8 bits for your hosts, you have (2^8) or 256 IP addresses. If you're told that you have 55 IP addresses, you're either sharing a network with other people or you need to learn what your network administrator is drinking and get him to share.

It's not uncommon to see a host IP with a netmask attached, e.g., 192.168.1.5/24. This gives you almost everything you need to know about the local network; just get the default gateway and you're on the Internet!

Netmasks and BGP

Your network must be a /24 or larger to route BGP, but what if it's larger? It is preferable to announce as few blocks as possible, in order to reduce the size of the global routing table. Multiple consecutive "class C" blocks might very well be a legitimate network block. You probably don't want to break out your calculator and transform all your network blocks into binary to find out, though! Here are some hints to determine whether a block of IP addresses is a legitimate single block.

Remember that network blocks are issued in multiples of two. This holds true all the way up the scale, including the larger network numbers. This means that each legitimate block must be a multiple of two. If a block is actually legitimate, it will be a multiple of its own size. For example, the address block 192.168.4.0–192.168.5.255 is a single contiguous range of addresses; and it's certainly two /24 networks, but is it a single legitimate network block? If this was a legitimate /23 network, we could fit additional /23 networks precisely into the 192.168 network. 192.168.0.0/23 fills 192.168.0.0 through 192.168.1.255, and 192.168.2.0/23 fills 192.168.2.0 through 192.168.3.255. Our 192.168.4.0 block picks up right there without any space left over, so it's a legitimate block! You can write this as 192.168.4.0/23, and you can announce it via BGP.

On the other hand, look at the block 192.168.32.0–192.168.96.255. This is a block of 64 consecutive /24 networks, or possibly a single /18 network. If it's a legitimate /18, we could fit an even multiple of 64 /24s into 192.168 before we reach this particular block. The very first block we would try, 192.168.0.0 through 192.168.64.255, overlaps the first half of our block. We can call this range two /19 networks, however: 192.168.32.0/19 and 192.168.64.0/19, which is better than announcing via BGP our 64 /24 networks!

INDEX

debugging logging level, 115
default routes for private connections, 47
delays in HSRP, 97
demarc points, 55
descriptions for interfaces, 24, 27
destination IP addresses
   in ping tests, 52
   for private connections, 45–46
dir command, 71, 74
disabling broadcast pings, 28
disaster recovery, 74
disk content in IOS upgrades, 71
domains for SSH, 109
dropped packets
   in ping tests, 52
   in traceroute tests, 53
DST (Daylight Saving Time) in NTP, 113
duplex setting, 26–27

E

emergencies logging level, 115
enable command, 10
enable mode, 10
enable passwords, 105
enable secret passwords, 105
encapsulation
   in interfaces, 24–25, 30
   for Internet connections, 36
encryption service for passwords, 104
equipment for private connections, 40
erase flash command, 73
error messages for router crashes, 50
error types in debugging information, 58–59
errors logging level, 115
Ethernet interfaces, 25–29
Ethernet IP addresses, 37
exclamation points (!) in ping tests, 52, 62
EXEC mode, 10–11

extended demarcs, 55
extended pings, 59–63

F

facilities, 116
failures, network. *See* network failures
finger service, 17
firewalls, 37
flash cards, 72
frame input errors, 59
front door passwords, 104
full routes setting in BGP, 77

G

gateways, 45–46
giant packets, 58
Google search engine, 3–4
greater than sign (>) prompt, 10

H

hardware platform, 7, 14
hashed passwords, 105
HDLC (High-level Data Link Control) protocol, 30
headquarters routing for private connections, 46–47
help, 11–12
host addresses, 120
hostnames
   in configuration, 17
   for SSH, 109
HSRP (Hot Standby Router Protocol), 94
   authentication in, 97–99
   and BGP, 98–99
   delays in, 97
   interface tracking in, 96–97
   operation of, 94–95
   preemption in, 96, 100
   testing, 99–100
   tuning, 96
hubs, 25
HyperTerminal program, 5–6

THE LINUX ENTERPRISE CLUSTER

Build a Highly Available Cluster with Commodity Hardware and Free Software

by KARL KOPPER

The Linux Enterprise Cluster explains how to take a number of inexpensive computers with limited resources, place them on a normal computer network, and install free software so that the computers act together like one powerful server. The book includes information on how to build a high-availability server pair using the Heartbeat package, how to use the Linux Virtual Server load balancing software, how to configure a reliable printing system in a Linux cluster environment, and how to build a job scheduling system in Linux with no single point of failure.

JANUARY 2005, 456 PP., $49.95 ($69.95 CAN) W/CD
ISBN 1-59327-036-4

THE BOOK OF WEBMIN

...or How I Learned to Stop Worrying and Love UNIX

by JOE COOPER

A comprehensive guide to UNIX system administration with Webmin, the Open Source system administration tool. Everything you need to know about Webmin's unique features, including the standard system features (network configuration, disk configuration, users and groups, etc.) and how to integrate the most popular services (Apache, BIND, Sendmail, and more). Tutorials show how to accomplish common tasks with each service.

JULY 2003, 312 PP., $34.95 ($52.95 CDN)
ISBN 1-886411-92-1

PHONE:
800.420.7240 OR
415.863.9900
MONDAY THROUGH FRIDAY,
9 A.M. TO 5 P.M. (PST)

EMAIL:
SALES@NOSTARCH.COM

WEB:
HTTP://WWW.NOSTARCH.COM

FAX:
415.863.9950
24 HOURS A DAY,
7 DAYS A WEEK

MAIL:
NO STARCH PRESS
555 DE HARO ST, SUITE 250
SAN FRANCISCO, CA 94107
USA

UPDATES

Visit **http://www.nostarch.com/cisco.htm** for updates, errata, and other information.